drive to
THRIVE

USING POSITIVE MOMENTUM
TO CREATE CHANGE IN YOUR LIFE

drive to
THRIVE

LAUREL RENKERT

Copyright © 2023 by Laurel Renkert

All rights reserved.

No part of this publication may be reproduced or transmitted in any form or by any means, electronic or mechanical, including photography, recording, or any information storage and retrieval system, without permission in writing from the author.

Requests for permission to make copies of any part of the work should be sent to the publisher.

This publication is not intended to be a source of medical or health advice. The information and interventions discussed in this book should not be used as a substitute for the advice of an accredited health professional.

Published and distributed by Merack Publishing

San Diego, USA

www.merackpublishing.com

Library of Congress Control Number: 2023912177

Renkert, Laurel

Drive to Thrive:
Using Positive Momentum to Create Change in Your Life

ISBN: 978-1-957048-94-9

DEDICATION

This book is dedicated to the girls who want to choose their own path: **BE BRAVE**.

This book is dedicated to the women who want to change course: **YOU CAN**!

CONTENTS

Prologue	1
Introduction	5
CHAPTER ONE The Upward Spiral	13
CHAPTER TWO Paying Attention	35
CHAPTER THREE [IM]perfect	43
CHAPTER FOUR Take Control of Your Health	49
CHAPTER FIVE Take Control of Your Relationships	73
CHAPTER SIX Take Control of Your Finances	87
CHAPTER SEVEN Take Control of Your Time	103
Conclusion	119
Epilogue	125
Eating Disorder Support & Resources	127

ACKNOWLEDGMENTS

ABOUT THE AUTHOR

PROLOGUE

Do you have a defining moment in your life?

You know, one of those moments that is seared into your brain because, looking back, you can see that it was pivotal?

I do.

When I was twenty years old, I was so sick that I dropped out of college. I came home for the summer and wasn't able to go back to school for over a year. College was an eye-opener for me, a harsh affirmation that I wasn't really special. I was ordinary. And this realization (combined with other elements—being away from home for the first time, being on campus with men, and not feeling desirable) created the perfect storm that caused a desperate need to take control of my life.

You might think that dropping out of college was the game-changing moment for me. It wasn't.

When I came home that summer, I barely saw my eighteen-year-old brother. We had been really close growing up, but this version of me was likely a stranger to him. I would go to work, binge and purge, go to sleep, and wake up at noon. Work. Vomit. Sleep. Repeat. This was the cycle of my life, week after week.

In my free time, I would seek attention from guys, a parade of them. (Not always in a sexual way. I was a good girl).

I remember sitting on the floor in my bedroom with some random guy. He wasn't a serious boyfriend, just someone I worked with who could keep me company for a while. As we were talking, I heard my brother walk up the stairs. He came into my room, looking visibly upset. He glared at the guy—someone he'd never seen before—and growled, "Get out of my house. Laurel is not okay. She is *not* okay. You need to go."

That was the first time I had ever seen my brother step outside of his comfort zone. I suddenly understood how much he cared for me, and how much I was hurting him.

My brother had never mentioned my eating disorder, so I'm not sure he knew exactly what was going on. But he is an intuitive human who knows me. The happy, joyful Laurel he remembered was not who I was at that time of my life, and he knew that something was terribly wrong. My brother is not the type of person to intervene unless a situation is very serious. He's also not an overly emotional guy.

Years earlier when our parents got divorced, I was dramatically affected, but my brother was like, "Okay." Maybe it was his age and he was too young to understand, or maybe being a boy, he processed differently. But my world was crumbling in the midst of my parents' break-up, and I wanted to protect him from the pain.

When he stormed into my room that day, he was so vulnerable, and I could clearly see that my actions had a negative impact on him. He was scared for me. I had always been the one who looked out for him, but in this moment, the script was flipped. He became my protector.

For the first time, I fully understood that the control I thought I had over my life had spiraled into self-destruction. I was hurting myself, and I was hurting others.

Something had to change.

INTRODUCTION

I grew up surrounded by mountains in the beautiful city of Anchorage, Alaska, where I had a typical, happy childhood. Life wasn't perfect, but it was pretty great. (What child of the '90s didn't have divorced parents, after all?) Mine was an outdoor family. I wouldn't say that we enjoyed hardcore tent camping (this was pre-glamping times; no yurts to speak of), but we certainly traveled around our state, hiking and appreciating nature.

Our neighborhood felt really safe. We lived on 20th Avenue, and another family—our closest friends—lived on 19th Avenue, and we kids would go back and forth with freedom. This family had a boy and a girl of similar ages to me and my brother. I have many fond memories with them, especially from summer. Summertime in Alaska is very short and precious, and we made the most of it.

The four of us would play cards outside, ride bikes, and climb the rocket at Valley of the Moon Park. The girls (both of us were the older siblings) would create obstacle courses for the boys to race on, and we would make them do silly contests and "brain games" all the time. We'd play in mud puddles, and jump on the neighbor's trampoline. Sometimes our families would drive up to Fairbanks (a short eight-hour jaunt) for a soccer tournament. Fairbanks had an "amusement park," if you can even call it that. "Alaskaland" (so original, right?) didn't have much to offer except a little choo-choo train that kids could ride in endless circles around the outer edge of the park. It probably had mini-golf too…we loved it.

Much of my childhood involved sports—soccer, running, skiing. A natural leader and athlete, I was a big fish in a small pond who was driven by any sort of achievement: sports, grades, clubs…if I was involved, I excelled. While I felt like a bright and shiny star in my small town, I knew that if I really wanted to test my potential, I would need to think bigger. In my senior year of high school, I decided that I wanted to go away for college—to the "lower 48"—and be exposed to other ways of life, new experiences, and vast horizons.

After graduation, my "big move" took me to the small town of Walla Walla, Washington, where I attended Whitman College. Why in the world would a girl with newfound freedom choose Walla Walla, you ask? My college of choice was dictated by the fact that a) it was the closest plane flight away from home; and b) my high school ski coach had graduated from Whitman, and she was someone I completely idolized (and still do). Wanting to follow in her footsteps, I worked hard to earn a spot on the college ski team and make a home for myself at her alma mater.

College was super hard in every aspect, academically, socially, emotionally, and I lost myself there. It turned out,

Introduction

even at a small school like Whitman, I wasn't special. Everyone there was just like me—a high achiever, scholastically inclined, friendly, smart…I didn't expect to feel so invisible. There was no way I could be a leader when surrounded by other students who were better than me. I was no longer a big fish. I was a small fish in a small, overcrowded pond. My insecurities, along with the desire to perform well as a Division I athlete, led to a debilitating eating disorder that sent me spiraling into self-destruction.

I left Whitman after two challenging years and checked myself into a treatment center in Arizona. My parents made every financial sacrifice—including money that had been allocated for my education—to pay for this life-saving intervention. I had been in a downward spiral for quite some time and had no control over my life or my health. Continuing down the path I was on was a sure death—although it didn't seem that dramatic at the moment. By the time I went to inpatient treatment, I truly wanted to put in the work to heal my brain and my body.

As I was preparing to leave after completing my final days of treatment, I received a phone call from my mom. With love and anguish, she informed me that when I returned to Anchorage, I would not be allowed to move back home.

"You've got to do your own thing," she said. "You need to find your own place and take charge of your recovery. We will be here for you, but it's time for you to take control of your life."

It was exactly the tough love angle I needed at the time, but it was terrifying. I was twenty-one years old, with no job, no money, no college degree, and no place to live. Deep down, I knew I couldn't go back home because I would fall back into old habits. Something had to change. So, I found a place to live, found some roommates (on Craigslist, how scary), and began to pick up the pieces of my life.

I white-knuckled it during the first few weeks. Everything felt hard. And daunting. Then one day, as I was driving to the nearest coffee shop to look on the internet for jobs, I felt something was missing. It was the heavy sense of dread and crippling fear about how I was going to pay my bills. It was gone! And it was replaced with clarity and, dare I say, conviction. I knew I could re-enroll in school and that I would figure out a way to pay for it. For the first time in a long time, I was in control of my future—in the driver's seat, both literally and figuratively.

My mom's difficult and brave decision, which forced me to take control of my life, created an opportunity for me to believe in myself, to feel empowered, and to gain the confidence I had been lacking for so many years. I was proud of myself for figuring out how to survive.

THE CURSE OF PERFECTIONISM

I think many women can relate to the disempowerment of being in the passenger seat—feeling out of control and letting fear dictate their choices. I wasn't very brave in the decisions I made early in my life, but I wonder if that is typical for a lot of young girls. I think it's a cultural thing. I was raised with supportive parents and amazing teachers, yet I found myself staying small, stifled by goals that were directly in line with societal expectations: go to a good college, earn top grades, be a good girl. While there is certainly nothing wrong with these expectations, they took away the creativity and inspiration of imagining my future. I simply couldn't see other options.

Growing up in Alaska offered a limited worldview. I thought I needed to follow the path of the women around me, women I looked up to. They were positive role models, who helped me achieve my goals, but in truth, the goals were not always authentically mine. When you are not exposed to new people, new places, or new ideas, how can you possibly envision a different way of living?

While my goals were small and my thinking limited, I became obsessed with shining brightly within those confines. I didn't want to be like every other girl in my town. I wanted to be as close to perfect as possible. If you haven't caught on yet, I'm a classic Type A personality! I used to see things as pretty black and white, good or bad, which is a very hard way to live.

In truth, most of my perfectionism was self-imposed. While I was hell-bent on earning straight A's in school, my parents were great about saying, "It's okay to get a B. We are proud of your hard work and accomplishments—if that's what you want. But we'd rather you not be so stressed out all the time."

Regardless of its origins, my desire to be perfect was all-consuming. I became a slave to it. Black-and-white thinking leaves no margin for error. I couldn't possibly measure up to my own expectations.

It's funny (not ha-ha funny, more ironic) that my perfectionist tendencies have led me to pursue success in areas where my excellence can be tangibly measured—academics and sports. I even chose a career where you can literally log into a system and see how you rank against every other advisor!

It's no wonder I developed an eating disorder.

Perhaps *your* perfectionist tendencies manifest in another way—anxiety, depression, stress, feeling constantly overwhelmed or like a failure. The parameters we build for ourselves (or that society constructs for us) are really limiting our beliefs about what we deserve—happiness, relaxation, tranquility. **We deserve to live a life we feel in control of and one that deeply satisfies us.**

The moment my mom handed me the steering wheel and said, "It's time to take control" was the moment I realized I could take whatever road I wanted. It changed my trajectory forever. No one but me was in charge of my life, my career, my health, and my happiness.

Look, I'm not an expert on how to live an incredible life, and I don't always have it together. Full disclosure, I've tried to write three different books and never made it past the first chapter. I discredited myself as being under-qualified before I even started. Self-sabotage is real!

Over the years, I've gained experience as a business owner, a wife, and a mother. While I have some credibility, I think my newfound confidence comes from knowing that I have a success story to share. Perhaps some of the lessons I've learned can help someone else. I'd love it if something I've learned and lived through can serve to make your life a little bit easier, more fun, more fulfilling, more colorful.

Deep down, I believe we are all on this journey together, we are all connected. Maybe in finally making a commitment to finishing this book, I can prove to myself that my dreams aren't grandiose. I hope this book can propel both you and me into the future and open us up to dreams we don't even know we want to achieve yet. How cool would that be?!

The thing is, neither you nor I can achieve those dreams by sitting in the passenger seat and letting life pass us by. We need to put ourselves in the driver's seat and take control of the journey that is our **one unique life.**

And, once we take the wheel and become the driver, we can roll down the windows, crank the tunes and enjoy the ride. After all, what is the purpose of life if not to experience moments of immense joy?

CHAPTER ONE
THE UPWARD SPIRAL

I assume you were drawn to this book because you are looking to make changes: to take control and live a life that fulfills you. Before you can make tactical adjustments to your everyday living, we need to talk about mindset. If you are caught up in a downward spiral, chances are you lack the confidence to take charge.

The first step is to become aware. Without awareness, change is impossible. Noticing when you have negative thoughts or when your healthy habits start to slide is what allows you to make the necessary adjustments. The more you lean into your awareness, the easier it becomes to respond quickly, to the point where it almost becomes second nature. That's the really cool thing about momentum—it can lift you up or pull you down, but you get to decide which direction it's going.

> **So, let's begin this journey at the starting line and project you into a spiral that takes you upward toward happiness.**

We've all found ourselves in a downward spiral at some point. If you don't have control somewhere in your life, everything feels negative. You might feel like you are on a treadmill (or perhaps a hamster wheel)—moving constantly, but going nowhere. The downward spiral affects how you feel about the quality of your life and has a huge impact on your general happiness.

Extracting yourself from the downward spiral might seem overwhelming, but it's not about making enormous changes. It's actually the opposite. The key to escaping the negativity is making many small changes, which slowly but surely help you regain control.

If you find yourself in a toxic work environment, it's probably not feasible to up and quit your job, but maybe you can change your schedule so you don't have to work with Joe Schmoe, who is the absolute WORST to be around. Tiny improvements add up to making bigger changes in your day-to-day and lead to a happier existence.

Maybe the changes you attempt fail the first time around. Don't give up! You might be trapped in an unhealthy romantic relationship, and you've already tried to leave seven times. My guess is that each time you've worked up the courage but have "failed," you've learned something about yourself and what you need to do in order to be fully prepared. Every famous person, every successful entrepreneur, has an origin story where they had 100 auditions and never got the part, or filed twenty patents before one went anywhere. Sometimes, that's our reality. You need to stick with it and keep trying. Pack a bag and put it in the trunk of your car. Reach out to friends and family who might support you. Save a little money. One day, you will be ready to leave that relationship because you've worked hard to build a safety net.

I want you to wake up feeling like each morning is a gift, as opposed to a curse, or even worse…feeling nothing at all. If you are currently feeling depressed and powerless, know that escaping the downward spiral is the result of a hundred little choices (and perhaps finding the right medication).

There's a lot of negativity in the world. What I've found is that for every downward spiral, there is an equally powerful upward spiral. Once you get a little taste of optimism and control, you can use that momentum to propel yourself forward and upward toward something greater.

THE UPWARD SPIRAL

You know that feeling when you've had a really great day—when everything seems joyful and in alignment, when possibilities seem like they are totally achievable, when you feel like you are absolutely on your A game? What if you could harness that feeling and repeat it consistently?

You can! It's called getting in the upward spiral.

An upward spiral, as defined in the Merriam-Webster dictionary, refers to "a situation in which something continuously increases."

Author and neuroscientist Alex Korb, PhD, describes the upward spiral as a series of small, actionable steps a person can take to rewire their brain and move toward a "healthier, happier life."

Arguably the most notable author to use the term "upward spiral" is Stephen R. Covey. You may have heard of a little book he wrote, called *The 7 Habits of Highly Effective People*[1]. Covey explains that the upward spiral consists of three components, which create change and growth: **learn, commit, do.**

I agree with both Korb and Covey (who would argue with Stephen R. Covey?!), and I have come up with my own version—a guiding question that has changed the way I move through my life.

> **How can I be intentional in setting up my day so that there are things I consistently look forward to?**

---

1 Covey, Stephen. The 7 Habits of Highly Effective People. New York, NY: Free Press, 1989.

If you are a business owner, a parent, or simply a human being in this world, many aspects of our day are out of our control. Having a family really taught me about letting go and inspired a huge shift in priorities for me. It's about knowing when to grab the wheel and when to sit back and enjoy the ride.

When I first discovered the upward spiral as a girl in my twenties, I was obsessive about it. I used to write down what I ate every day and how much exercise I got (not healthy!). I would keep a checklist of how I spent my time, how productive I was. As a mother, and generally a wiser woman, I have become slightly more relaxed (okay, okay, a lot more relaxed). My upward spiral is as simple as that first cup of coffee in the morning. My goal is to carve out mental space to sit and enjoy something as small as a warm mug in my hands.

The upward spiral is about intentionally seeking five minutes, multiple times a day, to calm you down, ground you, and bring you joy. It's a feeling of pride at the end of the day, **Wow! I helped someone today. I made a meal for my family. I went for a walk.** As you fall asleep feeling good about yourself and your life, you can use that momentum to propel you forward into the next day.

ACTIONS THAT PROPEL YOU UPWARD:

- Wake up thirty minutes earlier to have your coffee in silence before your family gets up and the chaos begins
- Listen to your favorite music in the car during your commute
- Go outside for fresh air on your lunch break
- Treat yourself to your favorite goody from the local bakery
- Spend thirty minutes unsubscribing from emails
- Write a thank-you note or send a card for no reason
- Express gratitude and notice blessings

Truthfully, you are not going to feel the inspiration every day. Some days are neutral, and it takes work to move into the upward spiral.

What I love about the spiral is that it is not a straight, organized, upward trajectory. It is swirly and messy. Sometimes there are slow swirls, which take a wide orbit and feel like a plateau. Other times, the swirls are tight and fast, projecting us into the stratosphere. I want to normalize the fact that growth is not evenly paced. Some days (weeks… months…) are simply better than others.

In most cases, we are our own worst enemy. This is actually good news. Seriously! It means our mindset is totally within our control. If we get better at identifying when negative thoughts creep in, or when we start to feel out of sync, we can take action.

I love the word "congruent" because it's a mathematical term that applies to so much more than math. (Yes, I know my inner geek is showing.) What it means to me is that the way we behave and the thoughts we have are in alignment. When we are positive, we treat others well because we feel good inside. When we are negative, we hurt, and we hurt other people. If you want to live in the upward spiral, you need to feel good about yourself. While great habits are crucial, it's equally important to recognize when you are starting to slip into the downward spiral. When I notice my thought patterns have taken a detour off the highway and have taken an unexpected turn onto a dark and bumpy road, I stop and reflect on my habits.

> **BEWARE OF YOUR
> LESS-THAN-BEST SELF! ASK:**
> - Am I spending too much time on social media?
> - How have I been sleeping?
> - Have I moved my body lately?
> - When was the last time I went outside?

In treatment, I learned the acronym HALT.
    H - hungry
    A - angry
    L - lonely
    T - tired

If one of these factors is influencing your current state, it is very difficult to show up as the best version of yourself. If you do a quick scan of your body and your mindset, you may find that one of these factors is at play. Then at least you are aware and can arguably do something about it. (It's also possible that *all* of these factors are at play, in which case I recommend brushing your teeth and going to bed immediately.)

I've learned through trial and error that building multiple brain breaks into my day is a great way to keep myself in the upward spiral. To clarify, scrolling your social media feeds is not considered a brain break! The purpose of a brain break is to nourish your body and your mind. Eat something healthy. Step outside for some fresh air. Get out of your chair (bonus points if you do some squats).

Humans aren't wired to work for eight or ten hours straight (though the current hustle culture might try to tell us otherwise). You need to take control and make adjustments that improve your daily experience. That way, when someone cuts you off on the commute home, you won't absolutely lose your mind! Perhaps instead of cursing that driver out, you might choose to wave instead of saluting them with your middle finger.

Having road rage doesn't serve you. There are a lot of bad drivers out there, and there always will be. Being in the upward spiral gives you a moment between stimulus and response to decide who you want to be. You might even give that bad driver the benefit of the doubt. Maybe that person is rushing home for a family emergency. Maybe their wife has just gone into labor. (Okay, admittedly, I put that one in there because as I write this chapter, I am *very* pregnant with my second child.) It's all to say that when we are in the upward spiral, and our mindset is congruent with our actions, we tend to give others a little more grace.

My suggestion is to write down ten to twelve action items and put them in a mason jar. Then, on the days when you are feeling the mental fatigue, you can easily pull an idea out of the jar and then take five to ten minutes to execute that suggestion. You may not initially feel excited about it, but I urge you to make a commitment to follow through. It takes effort to eject yourself from the downward spiral, but you will thank yourself afterward.

I'm about to introduce you to a few strategies I use to keep myself in the upward spiral. Throughout the book, you'll see these strategies unpacked in the context of each chapter, coupled with tactical action items for implementing in your own life. By sharing my story, my greatest hope is that you can find inspiration to make small changes, which will propel you toward the upward spiral.

Let's begin with a 30,000-foot view before we get granular.

1. The Gap and the Gain

I know what it feels like to struggle just to get out of bed. Some days, and in some seasons of life, it's really hard. We can easily fall into the pattern of being a robot, going through the motions, trying to get through the day. That's not living in the upward spiral. It's a flatline. Gaining upward momentum is a choice. It is not a passive mindset. Even on the hardest days, if you choose a growth mindset, you can look back and see how far you've come—maybe not in that moment, or on that day, but in general and over the course of time.

Renowned author and founder of Strategic Coach,™ Dan Sullivan talks about "the gap and the gain," a concept that radically changed how I saw my life.

Most of us look forward to the next major milestone because we were raised in a culture of goal setting and achievement. While believing there is no limit to your success and potential is motivating, constantly reaching for the next best thing can actually become detrimental to your mental health. No matter what you achieve, there is always something higher and better to strive for.

Dan Sullivan teaches us to flip the perspective 180 degrees and look backward. Compare where you are now to where you've been. When you measure backwards, your progress becomes as clear as day. You can see how you've grown and improved your life. It's much easier to feel positive when you reflect on how much you have gained. The proof that you *can* achieve propels you into the upward spiral.

We fall into the pit of despair—or "the gap" as Sullivan calls it—when we start comparing ourselves to others[2]. **This is taking too long. It's too hard. My colleague is more successful.** When we believe our own negative mindset, we are living in the gap instead of focusing on the gain. Another valuable lesson I learned in treatment: compare = despair.

Rather than being a victim of your own comparisons and getting pulled into the gap, doesn't it feel more empowering to focus on the small successes you've already had and use them as fuel for the fire, driving you toward the next road marker?

2. Delayed Gratification

Don't you love it when you order something on Amazon and it arrives on your doorstep the same day?! Technology is amazing! (Except for us Alaskans, who are too far off the grid for same-day delivery). The downside is we now live in a world where we have developed an insatiable appetite for instant gratification. Anything that requires patience—and doesn't arrive on our front porch right away—now feels like a disappointment.

Instant gratification, while very gratifying (Do you see what I did there?) actually detracts from the joy we are able to experience in the present moment. We have misinterpreted our wants as needs, and not only do we "need it," but we need it NOW. This impatience pulls us into the

---

[2] Sullivan, Dan. The Gap and The Gain: The High Achievers' Guide to Happiness, Confidence, and Success. Carlsbad, California: Hay House Business, 2021.

downward spiral. Instant gratification essentially robs us of the immense satisfaction that comes from working diligently on and staying dedicated to a long-term goal.

One of the exercises you can do to stay in the upward spiral is to intentionally practice delayed gratification.

Delayed gratification helps adjust our expectations so that they become grounded in reality. We can't expect something amazing to happen overnight. For example, if your goal is to climb the corporate ladder, that process might take years. That's not to say you can't celebrate small victories along the way. If we can set short-term attainable goals that are directed toward the BIG audacious dream, then that not only keeps us on track but meets our expectations of being rewarded. The ripple effect is that the joy of being rewarded increases the endurance of our long-term patience.

I like to gamify delayed gratification so that it feels fun instead of being a downer of an exercise. For example, on my morning commute, I try not to drink my coffee until I merge onto the freeway. It's only a seven-minute drive, which makes it a totally achievable goal. By waiting to drink my coffee, I increase my patience and self-discipline. Then I celebrate my victory by taking that first, delicious sip of morning java. And, as intended, it feels like a game instead of a chore.

OTHER WAYS TO PRACTICE GAMIFIED DELAYED GRATIFICATION:

- Buy your favorite treat but don't eat it until the next morning (with your coffee)
- If you find $20 in the pocket of your coat, or lying on the street, keep it hidden and save it for a rainy day
- When reading your favorite book or watching your favorite show, stop at the cliffhanger and come back to it a few days later
- Plan a fun activity for next month, then enjoy the anticipation of waiting for the day to arrive
- Set the clock for a certain amount of continuous productivity (like folding laundry) then take a fifteen-minute break and do something fun

Wouldn't it be cool if we could also gamify our thoughts? Responding immediately and emotionally to a person or situation can be deeply gratifying in the moment, but can also lead to a sense of regret shortly thereafter. In between the stimulus and your response is a pause where you get to make a choice about how you react. Hang with me on this: What if you could gamify that pause by coming up with five possible reactions?

Let's imagine your boss walks into your office and says, "I need you to work late tonight."

You had plans, but your boss doesn't seem to care. This was clearly an instruction, not a suggestion or question. You. Are. Staying. Late.

Hypothetically, you could:

1. Tell your boss that your time and efforts should be appreciated. Quit, then storm out.
2. Do the work. Stay late. Be totally resentful.
3. Agree to stay late but spend your overtime secretly streaming your favorite show.
4. Throw your coffee cup at the boss' head.
5. See this as an opportunity to earn your boss' trust and respect.

Hopefully, the gamification process breaks the tension by making you laugh at the ridiculousness of some of the options. And, fingers crossed, you chose #5.

Going through this exercise in the moment takes practice. Truthfully, it's tough to react calmly when you are caught off guard. Maybe another option is simply asking your boss for time to consider their request. (Assuming that it actually *was* a request). Give yourself space to process and run through the options if at all possible.

Sometimes, we forget about the pause and, as a result, act in a way not reflective of our best selves. In these moments, try to give yourself a little bit of grace. Forgive yourself and course correct.

3. Coaching

One of the ongoing ways I try to show up as my best self is through coaching. It has become a theme throughout my entire life and in many aspects of my life.

There is something amazing about using someone else's expertise to make you better. Find someone who has already been where you are, or where you want to go, and let them show you the path to success.

I've relied upon coaches first as an athlete, but then later in life in the form of counseling, business coaching, and life coaching. There are leaders out there who can help you develop your relationships, your financial stability, your health, your mental wellness…yes, you could probably learn everything you need to know independently, but why not expedite the process by asking for help?

I recognize that some of these resources can be expensive and that affordability is a real issue for a lot of people. There are a ton of free resources online! Heck, this book is a form of coaching in and of itself.

You've essentially asked for help, simply by choosing this book. I certainly don't have all the answers, but as I share my experience, I hope to show you that you *can, should, and deserve to* take control of your life.

4. Return on Enjoyment

Striving for the upward spiral involves making conscious choices that affect your happiness. Those choices often involve a degree of delayed gratification, sacrifice, indulgence, or investment. It might cost some money to create an inspiring workspace, for example, but if being in a calming and beautiful environment helps you focus and feel creative, then the investment will be worth it. And, if it brings you joy on top of all that, then the return you are getting for the monetary cost is a fantastic investment!

Instead of considering the traditional Return on Investment—which is commonly known as ROI—I like to think about my Return on Enjoyment (ROE).

ROE applies to so many aspects of life, from money to environment, to adventure, to food, to self care. Will investing in a sixty-minute hike bring you joy that will last throughout the day, subsequently making you a calmer and happier person? 100% worth it! If treating yourself to a cookie after a long, hard day makes you feel satisfied and rewarded, then go for it! 100% worth it! But if that third cookie doesn't taste as yummy as the first one did, then your ROE has decreased, and perhaps you need to reconsider. Munching on junk food when it no longer brings you joy will pull you into a downward spiral of shame (and this, my friends, is a place I inhabited for far too long, and it robbed me of so much joy).

So, in addition to weighing the pros and cons, think about the ROE when you make decisions in your life, both big and small.

POSITIVE PROPULSION PRINCIPLES

Once you become fairly proficient at keeping yourself in the upward spiral, you might find that new possibilities and opportunities present themselves to you, without much effort. One day, you'll look around at your life and be in disbelief at how fantastic it has become. That's not to say you haven't worked incredibly hard (because you have!), but the fruits of your labor are now apparent, and your mindset is attracting other like-minded people to you.

The ultimate goal of the upward spiral is not to achieve a certain thing or arrive at a certain place. The goal resides within the journey itself—the constant movement forward, the continuous growth and improvement.

In my experience, most of us can be rocking it out in one aspect of our lives, but may be less than stellar in another lane. Leaning into the driving metaphor, there may be some journeys where you are as hyper-focused as an F1 race car driver, and other journeys where you are lazily looking out the window, going *"Oh, pretty flowers!"* The problem is, having one aspect of your life out of control can easily pull the car off the road and into the rough.

Over time I have come to learn that every facet of life is equally important in keeping me in the upward spiral. I encourage you to reflect on each aspect of your life, as I have done with mine. Thankfully I learned some hard (and valuable) lessons along the way, which I would love to share with you—if you are willing to listen.

As a financial planner, I spend a lot of my time talking to people about money, and I believe (scratch that, I *know*) that finances are not the only currency in life. The quality of your life is dependent upon many factors, and if one facet feels out of your control, it becomes easy for others to spiral as well. Happiness and success are complex ideas, so goals need to be broken down into tangible components if we are to achieve them. This book aims to do just that.

I believe the various components of our lives can act as propulsion principles—forces of motion that can drive you upwards toward positivity or force you downwards toward despair.

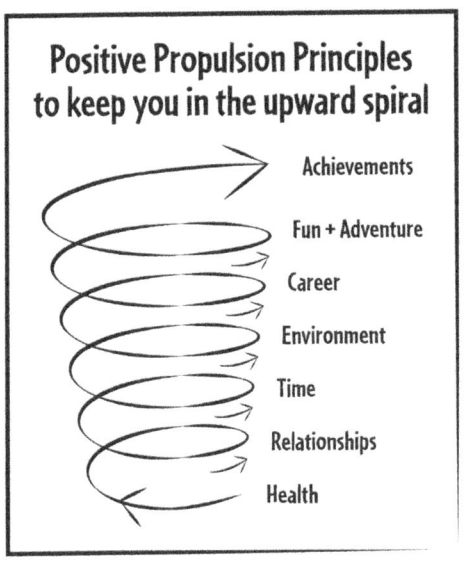

Let's take a moment to break down the language, as defined by the Oxford English Dictionary:

> **Positive**: constructive, optimistic, or confident
>
> **Propulsion**: the action of driving or pushing forward
>
> **Principles**: a fundamental truth that serves as the foundation of a belief or behavior or for a method of reasoning
>
> (As an aside, numerous mathematical principles form the laws of the universe. Shout out to math geniuses everywhere! You are my peeps!)

Now that we've briefly touched upon some of the strategies I use to keep myself in the upward spiral, let's step back and talk about the structure of the book itself. I want you to get the most out of reading this that you can, and I believe setting clear expectations is key to moving forward together.

Each chapter will unpack the positive propulsion principles, which guide me in certain aspects of my life. By maintaining awareness in each of these areas, I can stay within the upward spiral throughout the day. For the remainder of our precious time together, we will take a close look at:

- Health
- Relationships
- Finances and Career
- Time, Environment, and Adventure
- Achievements

At the end of each chapter, you'll find concrete suggestions for how to take control of your life, one of which (surprise, surprise) will be a numbers exercise!

YOUR LIFE BY THE NUMBERS

Nerd alert: I love numbers! Numbers don't lie to you. They are an unbiased measure of success.

In high school, math was the only subject where I could listen to music while doing my homework. Whatever distraction was around me, I could focus on the numbers because I was totally in my element.

I had an amazing calculus teacher, who encouraged me to lean into my math skills. She saw my talent and took extra care to nurture it. I began to see numbers in every aspect of my life. I was very athletic, and the connection between numbers and sports was obvious. Mathematically, you run 100 meters in a specific amount of time. There's no debating if you ran faster or slower than your competitor. Your success was measurable. In school, 98% on a test is undoubtedly higher than 92%. It's a bigger number and a better score. End of story. Today, I am a financial advisor, and numbers dictate the success of my business. I remember my first million-dollar client. It was a powerful experience, a monumental achievement.

Numbers are all around us. What is your relationship with the numbers on your bathroom scale? (If it's not a good one, throw that scale away). Do you have enough money to pay your bills? How many hours a day do you spend looking at a screen? How much time do you spend sitting? How often do you get out into nature? How much money do you need to retire comfortably?

One of my primary goals is to make this book actionable. I don't want this book to be all about me and my story (I'm pretty basic, after all). My greatest hope is that you can take something from the lessons I share and implement strategies to change your own life.

So, even though I am a young entrepreneur, a new(ish) mother, not an expert on happiness, and still learning to own my un-perfection, I hope this book can serve you. My greatest wish is that you walk away feeling inspired to jump into the driver's seat and steer directly toward the facet of your life that feels the most out of control. I want this book to provide a road map toward a better future and bigger dreams. I want you to step out of your comfort zone, change lanes if you feel like it, and know that you can lead a happy life.

CHAPTER TWO

PAYING ATTENTION

My dad is a hippie from Alaska, who wandered along the west coast and Hawaii throughout his twenties. He values minimalism and practices Buddhist ideals, and these concepts were pretty influential in my life from youth into adulthood. And philosophies that were fairly unusual in Alaska. (I would wager that not many of my peers were encouraged to engage in this type of thinking at such a young age).

While it was never my goal to reach enlightenment, some of the lessons my dad shared left an imprint: right thought, right speech, right action, right livelihood, right understanding, right effort, right mindfulness, right concentration.

Let's take the idea of *right thought*, for example. My dad was (and still is) big on non-attachment. It relates directly to expectations and to putting our struggles into perspective. Having non-attachment allows you to adjust your goals and experiences, to not get overly disappointed when something doesn't happen as planned. As a result, I learned to reframe failure at an early age. **Well, I wanted that thing and didn't get it, but I am alive and well. Was the loss truly devastating? No. It was disappointing, for sure, but I am not destroyed by it.**

My mom loves to use the phrase "disappointing, not devastating" as it relates to life's challenges. In most cases, the trials we go through are discouraging, but not catastrophic. She reinforced this idea to me and my brother, which allowed us to zoom out and believe that we would be okay, eventually.

Our successes come in fleeting moments, but so do our failures. Nothing lasts forever—good or bad. Everything comes and goes, everything ebbs and flows. We can be upset by our setbacks, but how much we suffer from them is a choice. The power of mindset will determine whether you give up control and become a victim, or take control of the situation and learn from it. (My parents are both in the field and business of psychology. These are the conversations we had at the dinner table when I was a kid. I mean, how do you explain the concept of *suffering* to an eight-year-old?!)

PAYING ATTENTION

My mom and dad both taught me the importance of right concentration. "Paying attention" is what they called it. Paying attention sounds like a simple task, but in reality, it's a challenging thing to do. Life is busy and hard, and we can easily slip into a mindless robot-zone. There are still days I drive to work only to realize I have no idea how I got there or if I ran a red light because my mind was elsewhere. I wasn't paying attention. That feels scary.

If you are able to go through your day reminding yourself to pay attention, then life instantly and automatically gets a little bit better. You will enjoy your food more when you sit down to eat lunch. You will notice the beautiful scenery when you drive to work. Relationships get a little easier.

Look, you can always find a reason to be grumpy, but wouldn't life be better if you found a reason to feel positive? Paying attention leads to gratitude and to more positive things occurring for you.

In order to pay attention, start by noticing all those tiny blessings that make up your day and try to pass that positivity along to others. See what comes of it!

In the building where I work, there is a woman who goes into the hallway every hour to do some exercise. I think it's totally awesome. For the longest time, I would shuffle past her, and she would apologize for getting in the way. Outside of this regular interaction, we never really spoke to each other. She was doing her thing, I was doing mine. We were busy. No big deal.

Then one day, she noticed I was pregnant and began chatting with me. I opened up and shared how inspirational I thought she was. Our daily interactions became more personal, and we now look forward to seeing each other. This budding friendship was the result of us finally paying attention to each other. Let the record show that she predicted I would have a boy. I had a girl.

Imagine how life would change if we all took time to notice each other, to try and think about things from someone else's perspective. What's that famous quote from *To Kill a Mockingbird*?

> "You never really understand a person until you consider things from his point of view...until you climb into his skin and walk around in it."
>
> ~ Atticus

I have no patience for people who are rude to employees in the service industry—for people who complain to their waiters, for instance. So often, we let those people fade into the background. They take our orders and our plates, and we don't look at them unless something is wrong. If you really stop to pay attention, you'll see that they are hustling around the restaurant, serving multiple tables, answering phones, talking to the kitchen, cleaning up spills. If you take a moment to notice how hard your waiter is working, maybe you will be a little kinder if there is a mistake in your order that needs to be corrected.

MASLOW'S HIERARCHY OF NEEDS

I see a lot of alignment between paying attention and Maslow's Hierarchy of Needs. Maybe like you, I learned about Maslow in seventh or eighth grade, and it totally blew my mind. It was one of the rare concepts I learned in school that actually made sense and felt really important (thanks again to my parents for their Psych 101 lessons at the dinner table).

If we are paying attention to the quality of our lives and taking control of the bottom layers of the pyramid, we can free ourselves from being in a survival state and propel ourselves into the upward spiral. When your health, finances, and relationships feel secure, your brain becomes free from worry. Now you have space for creativity and higher-level thinking. You can dream about adventures and strive toward achievement! When you have clarity of thought, your decisions become so. much. easier. **This will pull you into the downward spiral. That will carry you into the upward spiral.**

Two tools we will use in this book to help you create alignment and security at the bottom of the pyramid are the *Incompletes* List and the *Intolerables* List.

THE INCOMPLETES LIST

Many of us carry around an unconscious awareness of something that might be missing from certain aspects of our lives, issues that need to be brought into the conscious mind. In order to move into a state of awareness, you need to pay attention to what is bothering you. It requires time and energy to evaluate the different areas of your life and to decide what needs to be addressed.

I'll explain by sharing a story. A few years ago, something felt incomplete in my relationship with my dad. While it took me a while to figure out, I realized I had never thanked him properly for paying for my inpatient eating disorder treatment.

I knew a face-to-face conversation would not be the best option for either of us because it would make us both uncomfortable. So, I decided to write him a letter and give it to him on his birthday. That way, he could read it in private. My dad is a pretty sentimental guy. He saved (and laminated) many pieces of artwork that my brother and I made for him as kids, so I knew a letter would resonate with him. He could keep it and come back to it whenever he wanted to.

We never really talked about the letter, but I knew he appreciated it, and it felt as though I brought closure to that "incomplete."

Some years back, a wonderful business coach by the name of Doug Carter encouraged me to identify aspects of my life that felt incomplete. I want to give him credit for this amazing concept, as it was a game changer for me. Thanks to his brilliance and guidance, I can share this strategy with you today.

We all have some *Incompletes*—in our relationships, in our finances, in our health, in our unacknowledged dreams. At the end of most of the following chapters, you will find a (literal) space to do some reflecting. Are there any *Incompletes* in that area of your life? It may take time for you to pay attention long enough to notice them, but once you see the *Incomplete*, you are empowered to take action and rectify it.

THE INTOLERABLES LIST

Along with the *Incompletes* List, you will also find the *Intolerables* List as a personal reflection prompt. Let's be honest, while some things simply need to be addressed, others need to be fully removed. These might come in the form of toxic relationships, bad habits, or limiting beliefs.

Intolerables are where you draw your line in the sand (or in the snow if you are from Alaska). They are things that, from now on, you refuse to live with. *Intolerables* do not serve you. They will no longer impact your life or influence you in any way.

The *Intolerables* are important to consider because they essentially act as your boundaries, which we all know can be difficult to establish (and arguably even more difficult to maintain).

BE THE DRIVER

By actively reflecting on your *Incompletes* and *Intolerables,* and deciding to take action, you move out of victimhood. You stop blaming people and circumstances and begin to take control. When you decide to jump (or perhaps scooch) into the driver's seat, you head toward the upward spiral.

Moving beyond victimhood allows you to look back on your choices and realize you played a part in them all along. You can now identify where you went wrong and what you did differently. There's no shame in past mistakes. With knowledge and control, you can move toward a better outcome, a more positive tomorrow, and an amazing long-term future.

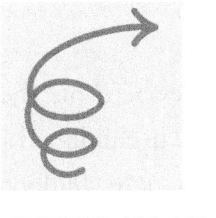

CHAPTER THREE

[IM]PERFECT

You may have already guessed it, but my hope is that the words I write inspire you to take control of your life, and here is where we need to pause…

The word "control" has been given a bad rap. Especially as women, we can be branded as *control freaks*, a term that is not meant to be endearing. I want to free us from that negative connotation by reminding us all that "control" is not a dirty word!

We all fall on a spectrum of control, ranging from those of us who feel as if life is happening to us (without our consent or input) to those—like me—whose control issues stem from the constant pursuit of perfection. Neither end of the spectrum is healthy, but I do believe there is a sweet spot—an aspect of control that empowers you (but not in a white-knuckled, I-need-to-be-in-control-of-all-the-things-all-the-time kinda way).

THE SPECTRUM

We are all born somewhere on the spectrum of control, tendencies that emerged in childhood and were either squashed or encouraged. Think back to childhood and try to recall what you fought for control over. Maybe you were a picky eater, or you were particular about what your clothes looked like. How were those bids for control met by the adults in your life?

When I was young, I was very particular about many things, and one of them was the bumps in my socks. It was like *The Princess and the Pea*! I couldn't focus if I felt the toe seam against my skin. I also refused to play in the sandbox because I didn't like the feeling of dry, sandy hands. My parents respected my sensory sensitivities and took a nonchalant approach. They let me make choices about what kind of socks I wanted to wear and where I wanted to play. In essence, they empowered me to make decisions about my own body.

Spoiler alert: This need to micromanage my body spiraled during my college years. When other aspects of my life felt untethered and undesirable, I grasped for a sense of control wherever I could and held on tightly. Too tightly. I needed to learn how to loosen my grip and let things unfold as they may.

If, like me, you've ever fallen on one end of the control spectrum or the other, you may have felt the detrimental effects. When you fight for too much control, it takes you out of the present moment. You are constantly thinking ahead, anticipating, and planning. If you feel helpless and totally out of control, you can get stuck in a perpetual cycle of indecision or victimhood.

What I've learned over the years is that there is a freedom in channeling control in a positive way. It's about finding balance because life will always be a push-pull. You will need to learn what you can control and what you need to let go of. Maybe you can't control the fact that you have a colleague you don't like, but you *can* choose not to walk by their office, and avoid having to see them. Instead of falling into the downward spiral, you can recognize which elements of the situation are within your ability to choose. You can even make a game of it! How many hours can you go without running into that irritating coworker?! Two hours? That's a win! Four hours? Even better! Now, you are moving toward the upward spiral.

Sometimes, we just need a little grease to get the ball rolling—a small moment of control and choice to shift our momentum. Maybe it's not a coworker, but your actual job that you don't like. Perhaps you cannot afford to quit and this feels out of your control, but you *can* choose to leave the house fifteen minutes earlier to buy a yummy coffee before work. And, as you are driving to the café, take (and make) time for gratitude. You have a car. You can afford a latte. The taste of that sweet-sweet milky caffeine is divine! Once your mindset becomes more positive, you might even start imagining ways to increase your education or experience and start to work toward finding other employment.

See? It's a ripple effect.

[IM]PERFECT

We often need to be our own inspiration. No one else is in charge of your mindset, and no one else can change it.

Even though I've come a long way, I still struggle with perfectionism daily. I have to constantly remind myself what areas of life I can control and which areas I clearly need to make peace with. I can't tell you how many times I've wished I didn't have to make so many decisions in a day, that someone would just tell me what to do at work. I don't *actually* want this. What I want is to save some brain power and not feel so exhausted. This is ultimately why I brought on a business partner and built up a team. When I finally let go of the need to control and do everything myself (with total perfectionism), I was able to relax.

For a long time, I let my need to be *perfect* get in the way of being *great*. If I couldn't be the best, I was afraid to try. This not only cost me a sense of calm, but robbed me of fun, adventurous opportunities. I was always training, studying, exercising, and counting calories. Now, after gaining some wisdom and becoming a mother of two tiny humans who deserve my time and attention, I've even learned not to let *great* become the enemy of *good*. If it means I get to spend more time with my family, sometimes *good* is good enough.

I'm not perfect. I am perfectly imperfect—someone who gets exhausted trying to do it all. In order for me to remain in control of my life in a healthy way, I am willing to ask for help. No woman is an island, and you don't need to go it alone.

CONTROL SHOULD FEEL EMPOWERING

It's important to acknowledge that our ability to be in control will ebb and flow depending on the season of life we are in. Sometimes balance is about letting go, and other times it's about getting into that driver's seat. There will be times when you need to become hyper-focused on a goal and need to ignore other aspects of your life—relationships, free time, financial savings. The sacrifice, though, should serve the purpose and feel well worth it.

Control should never feel anxious, exhausting, or fearful. This book is not meant to advocate for control in a way that stresses you out, nor is it meant to shame you. It is about my wish for you to harness control of your life and channel it into something positive, in a way that empowers you and puts you in the upward spiral.

Control is not a dirty word. So, go ahead and grab it! You deserve it.

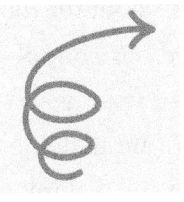

CHAPTER FOUR

TAKE CONTROL OF YOUR HEALTH

We're continuing this journey together by talking about health for two reasons:

One, I believe it is arguably *the* most important aspect of life to take control of. It is my number one value. If you don't feel good, if you have ever been injured or seriously ill, even if you are suffering from one hell of a headache, you simply cannot perform at your best or enjoy life to the fullest. Your health determines how you show up in the world. When you are physically, mentally, and spiritually well, you are a more understanding partner, parent, friend, and human. Foundationally speaking, caring for the health of your mind and body will keep you on the upward spiral.

Two, in full disclosure, this is probably the hardest chapter for me to write. Even though I am deeply committed to my own health, it has been a difficult road for me. I need to start here, to share my story with you.

As we dive into this chapter, I want you to know that I will strive to be sensitive about the topic of health. Sometimes, our health is not within our control—disease, mental illness, allergies—and if this is part of your story, please know that I empathize with you. We are all doing the best we can with the cards we are dealt. Even still, I think most of us can take small steps toward improvement, no matter the context.

MY STORY

Growing up, I would say I had a fairly average informal education about nutrition and health. My mom expected me and my brother to cook once a week—a meal that had to include a protein, some vegetables, and a starch. We were also in charge of preparing our school lunches with healthy food, so I always had some combination of a fruit, a bagel, and some trail mix. (In hindsight, this probably wasn't the most "healthy.")

My coaches would talk about the importance of nutrition and organize a carb-loading spaghetti feed for the athletes on the night before race days. Teachers would have discussions about puberty in health class, but it always felt very generic. I had a hard time connecting that information to my own body. There was so much I didn't know (like how to insert a tampon) and, like most middle schoolers, was too embarrassed to ask.

Most of us develop an awareness of our bodies during our middle school years. I grew up in the Abercrombie & Fitch era—my locker was decorated with photos of tall, thin white females and the ripped abs of white males. I began to realize my athlete's body looked nothing like those models, and there weren't many other examples in the media. I would go through phases of noticing body parts of other people—one month I noticed everyone's butts, the next I would fixate on noses. I don't know if this fixation can be considered normal for a pre-teen girl. *shrug* Please don't judge me.

When I was a junior in high school, I had a nasty track and field accident and chose not to compete the following season. So, instead of spending my time at the track, I joined the soccer team. I was still moving my body, but the output of exercise wasn't nearly the same. I was no longer running eight miles a day. This was the first time I realized there was a direct relationship between the input and output of calories. I couldn't keep eating whatever I wanted (my standard bagel and trail mix lunch wasn't quite cutting it).

When I transitioned to college, I decided to take a year off from all sports. I was pretty worried about the academic pressure and the transition of starting life in a new town. My life essentially went from being very structured with all of my high school activities, to zero infrastructure in college. As a result, I gained more weight.

College was so much more challenging than I expected. I had to work harder to achieve the level of excellence I had in high school. In my first semester, I didn't get straight A's (as I was accustomed to) even though I was doing everything I knew how to do. None of my study habits had changed, yet it wasn't enough now. This was the beginning of my downward spiral. I didn't have sports anymore. I didn't have perfect grades anymore. On top of that, many of my new friends had college boyfriends, but the boys didn't seem to be paying any attention to me.

After surviving my first year, I made the decision to get back into shape for the cross-country ski season. I was determined to make the Division I team. Around this same time, the possibility of rekindling an old flame emerged—someone I had been involved with in high school. I thought to myself, "The next time I see this guy, I want to look amazing." The downward spiral, combined with my perfectionism and need for control, created the ideal breeding ground for an eating disorder.

In the summer between my freshman and sophomore year, I exercised hard, ate really well, and lost some weight. People noticed and complimented my body. In reality, I had slimmed down to my former high school weight, but something in my mind had shifted. It wasn't enough. At first I thought, "I'll just eat these certain foods." Then, "I'll just cut back on my intake a little."

It was a fast descent down a slippery slope. I kept justifying my weight loss by telling myself I would stop once I reached my next goal, but then I didn't. I was trapped in a massive experiment on my own body. Maybe you can relate. **What if I ate less? What would happen if I threw up? Maybe I should try keto. I hear CrossFit is awesome.**

So-and-so likes Pilates, and perhaps I can give it a try. What is intermittent fasting?

Before I knew it, the identity I had in high school—athlete, leader, great student—had disappeared and was replaced with only one goal: be thin.

Everyone tells you that your first year of college is going to be epic. *It's going to be so much fun!* For me, it wasn't. It was downright hard. Coming back the second year, I was very focused and was grasping to regain control of my life. But nothing was ever good enough, and it spiraled quickly. By the end of my sophomore year, I was too sick to return to school.

Three of my closest friends organized an intervention where they bravely said, "Laurel, we know you are not okay." I am eternally grateful for these women. I know how hard it was for them to confront me, but it showed how much they cared. I love them to this day. They made me promise that immediately after arriving home for the summer, I would tell my mom how much I was struggling.

My parents and I hoped that being home from college would be positive for me, that a different environment would set me on a healthier path. We were wrong. Things got worse. The knowledge that I wasn't going back to school made me feel like a failure. I didn't know what my future held, and having so much up in the air didn't bode well for my perfectionism. (I'm sure you can imagine.)

I had no traction and was falling deeper and deeper into the downward spiral. I knew that I needed a significant amount of help. I stayed consistent with counseling and attended some local support groups, but I was still living at home and working (in a restaurant, ironically). My parents and I decided that getting better needed to become my only priority, so they conducted a ton of research and found an excellent treatment center.

On the day I arrived, I had no energy, no passion. My life felt like the nightmare version of the movie *Groundhog Day*. But, I truly wanted to change, to heal. I was grateful for a place where I could have a blank slate, where decision-making was taken away from me, and where healing became my number-one goal. I wanted to nourish my body and my mind. This marked the beginning of my lifelong road to recovery and the upward spiral that inspired writing this book.

That year, I spent Thanksgiving, Christmas, and New Year's in treatment. I was also there for my twenty-first birthday, where instead of toasting with my first legal glass of champagne, we toasted with shot glasses of Ensure. I missed a lot when I was in treatment. While my life stood still, the outside world carried on without me. But you know what? That was exactly where I needed to be at that time. It was the best decision for me.

THE LESSONS I LEARNED

I recently read a book called *Good for a Girl*, written by one of the greatest long-distance runners of my generation, Lauren Fleshman. She talks about the emotional and mental strain placed upon female athletes. Her story profoundly resonated with me.

I got to thinking about what message I would like to share with my daughter when she reaches that vulnerable middle school age, or what I wish my thirteen-year-old self would have known. This is what I would tell them:

> **As you grow, your body will change, and it will likely feel weird. But you are not unique, and you are not alone. If you are an athlete, puberty will make your body slower. You are going to have to train harder to stay at the same pace. This is not your fault. It's normal. Sometimes, you might feel alien in your own skin and frustrated with your body. Things may feel out of your control. All women feel this from time to time, and most of us find a happy ending on the other side of it. Be patient and be loving with yourself.**

As women, we are often fighting against our own bodies, especially during times of hormonal transition—during your period, pregnancy, and perimenopause. There is so much happening in your body and in your mind, which can make it an uncomfortable position (literally and figuratively) to be in. Whatever you can do to be at peace during those seasons should become your top priority. Pay attention to your thoughts and learn about what is happening inside your body. Most importantly, talk about what you are going through.

It has been amazing to see the culture of women athletes changing in recent years. Superstars like Simone Biles and Naomi Osaka are putting their mental health above competition. Their openness and vulnerability remind us that health is paramount to success, and that mind, body, and soul all need to be cared for.

Lastly, if you find your health suffering and you are being pulled into the downward spiral, it can be challenging to turn it around. I've been there. I know. When I hit rock bottom and turning inward was near impossible, I would write a note of gratitude to a friend to distract me from the tedious self-work I was doing. My dad likes to remind me to see others' joy as my own. When you feel as if there is nothing in your life worth celebrating, be happy for the success of those around you. If you can't see or feel your own joy, tap into someone else's. This mind-shift adjustment will shift the momentum, little by little. Taking action to change your mindset will eventually spill over into other areas of your life—fitness, nutrition, and even spirituality.

Although my eating disorder originated from my need to take control of my life, it very quickly got out of control. This is the nature of the illness—it relegates you to the passenger seat. Going to treatment was what finally put me back behind the wheel. While this was one of the most difficult experiences of my life, it gave me more appreciation for my health and made me mindful to keep it a top priority (not at all times, but at most times).

NUTRITION

Eating intuitively has been a struggle for me as an adult, so I've had to learn a lot about nutrition and what my body requires in order to feel good.

In America, we tend to value convenience over quality. We live very busy lives, and when it's 5:30 and the kids are screaming because they are hungry…we reach for fast food. The convenience is stated right in the name! It's quick, cheap, and delicious (to some). But it's not good for us.

I'm not a dietician, but one of the things I've learned about nutrition is that soft and spongy foods (like hamburger buns and fries) don't require a lot of energy for our bodies to break down. When food is in its raw, original form, it's dense, perhaps crunchy, and you need to chew it. Your body expends energy to break down the food and extract the nutrients. This was an "aha" moment for me, something I had never thought about before. I want my body to work hard to process the food I eat, to get the most fuel from it.

The closer we can get to eating food in its natural state, the better, which means anything manufactured or processed is not ideal. Let's take an apple, for example. You can eat a raw, crunchy apple. You could snack on some apple sauce. Or you could drink apple juice. Each choice is a little more processed and requires less energy to consume, and by the time we get to the juice (which is basically sugar water), you really don't reap any nutritional benefits at all.

Eating well, or even eating better, takes planning. In Alaska (where I live) we don't always have access to fresh, local, organic produce. Therefore, I need to supplement and cook with what is offered at the grocery store, most likely imported from Mexico. When we try to eat seasonally, it means we eat a lot of potatoes and carrots!

Here are some tips and tricks I've learned that helped me take control of my nutrition:

- Know what is available in your community
- Meal plan in advance
- Try not to eat out of boredom (remember your ROE!)
- Grocery shop on the perimeter of the store (that's where food is the freshest; everything in the middle aisles is processed)
- Try one new recipe a month
- Cook at home instead of eating out
- Buy smaller plates to assist with portion control
- Fill with ½ carbs, ¼ veggies, ¼ protein (btw, this DOES come from a dietician)
- Don't watch TV while you eat—it's best to be mindful during your meal, so you can sense when your body is full

MENTAL HEALTH

Whether you believe in a greater power or not, I think a component of our mental wellness comes from accepting that some elements of life are out of our control. You could wake up tomorrow and anything could happen! It can be so scary that it keeps you from getting out of bed…there are so many terrible possibilities! However, if you adopt a mindset that life is an adventure, and you want to be an active, loving, willing participant, the emotion can shift from fear to excitement.

There are numerous strategies we can adopt to help make peace with the unknown, to cope with the stress of life, and to care for our mental health. Perhaps you love getting into nature, which can be a deeply healing and spiritual experience. Maybe you belong to a church and find calm within a connected religious community. You can listen to incredible podcasts or read books that help you heal and encourage you to reflect. Go for a walk without the dog or the kids (and take another one with them). Step outside for five minutes during your workday and look at the sky.

Giving yourself *one hour* a week to focus on your mental health and spirituality is a blessing. I mean, there are literally 168 hours (over 10,000 minutes) in a seven-day span! I challenge you to carve out 60 minutes (that's only 0.6% of your week) to ground yourself. Give yourself the gift of a weekly mental health date and do something that brings you joy.

I know it's hard! We are all very busy, but if you don't allow yourself time to reflect on your thoughts, there is no space left for creativity. There is no space left for healing. You will be so busy making your mental grocery list or analyzing the argument you had with your spouse or your boss, that beautiful, meaningful thoughts can't even enter your brain! How do you expect to think of something new or positive if you're frantic all of the time?

When life gets too busy, my overwhelm tends to breed anxiety. My mind goes to the worst-case scenario. **I am not spending enough time with my kids. They feel unloved. I haven't eaten well this week. I am sabotaging my health. I haven't paid enough attention to my husband. My marriage is in trouble.** Instead of ignoring these dark thoughts, I shine a spotlight on them. I play them out in their entirety until I realize that those scary things will never come to fruition. In fact, they are usually ridiculous! They are not the truth; they are lies that creep into my brain when life feels out of control or when I am experiencing decision fatigue.

Women make so many decisions a day, it's no wonder our brains begin to fizzle. **What do the kids need to pack for daycare today? What should we eat for breakfast? If we leave ten minutes later this morning, can I still beat the traffic and make it to work on time? Do I need to answer that email immediately? Who can I ask to help me with that presentation?** And on, and on, and on it goes. Many of us feel responsible for ourselves, our families, our colleagues, and our friends, and this mental load can be exhausting. It becomes easy to fall out of balance.

PRO TIP: planning ahead can ease the heavy load. Pre-planning (and pre-cooking meals) removes a decision that is usually made at the end of a tiring day. Taking a few minutes the night before to choose your outfit, pack your lunch, and prep the coffee machine simplifies a busy morning routine.

FINDING BALANCE

Believe it or not, the countries that report the highest levels of life satisfaction boast short work days and extended vacations. Nordic countries such as Finland and Denmark are consistently amongst the happiest in the world[3]. Their secret? Work-life balance, or as a wise person once phrased it to me, life-work balance (life should come first, after all).

Many Asian countries value meditation as a means of focusing on their mental wellness. Research from the Mayo Clinic states that meditation is effective in combating stress and increasing overall relaxation[4]. It is linked to a reduction in anxiety and depression, lowers your heart rate and blood pressure, increases creativity, and improves sleep. If taking

---

3   https://www.cnbc.com/2020/01/09/are-danish-people-really-happy-nordic-work-life-balance-secrets.html
4   https://www.mayoclinic.org/tests-procedures/meditation/in-depth/meditation/art-20045858#:~:text=Meditation%20can%20give%20you%20a,centered%20and%20keep%20inner%20peace.

ten minutes out of your day to sit or walk silently with your thoughts has that many benefits, why aren't we all doing it?!

While we clearly have a lot to learn from other countries around the world, the good news is that the pendulum is swinging toward a strong mental health movement in America. We are beginning to normalize therapy, medication, and self-care. Remember that paying attention to the quality of our thoughts also keeps us in the upward spiral.

If you feel yourself slipping into the downward spiral, that's a signal for you to stop and assess how you are spending your time. Are you working too much? Are you getting outside? Are you spending time with your family? Are you moving your body?

The Global Health and Fitness Association shares a 2021 review of over 1000 studies conducted over the past thirty years. A whopping 89% of the literature describes a significant association between physical activity and mental health[5]! This is because the endorphins our bodies secrete during exercise help combat stress[6]. While the thought of going for a walk or attending an exercise class in the middle of the terrible day

---

5 https://www.ihrsa.org/improve-your-club/new-report-exercise-plays-key-role-in-mental-health-well-being/#:~:text=Out%20of%201%2C158%20studies%20examined,or%20exercise%20and%20mental%20health.
6 https://www.mhanational.org/what-are-endorphins#:~:text=Because%20endorphins%20help%20relieve%20stress,response%20to%20a%20stressful%20experience.

you are having might not sound appealing, you will definitely thank yourself afterward.

YOU CAN MOVE YOUR BODY AND MAKE IT FUN

If you want to live your best life, I absolutely recommend doing some sort of physical activity most days of the week. In a world of shortcuts, where we can drive or take the bus anywhere, we have stopped using our bodies like we used to. We no longer walk to the farm down the road for food (or churn our own butter), and our mental and physical health pays the price.

Exercise does not have to be tedious and dull. It can actually be enjoyable! Take your kid sledding and pull them up the hill. Go for a run and listen to a funny podcast or an audiobook. Dance in the kitchen. Take a boxing class. Jump on the trampoline. Everyone can find something that suits their lifestyle and their unique personality. There are lots of good-looking fitness instructors out there…just sayin'.

WAYS TO GAMIFY YOUR HEALTH...

- Instead of eating out when you are low on groceries, use what you have, add a dash of creativity, and try to create something yummy (check the freezer)
- Lean into delayed gratification and do ONE monthly dinner date (bonus: this saves money AND gives you something fun to look forward to)
- Challenge yourself to move your body for five minutes every hour during the work day (I recommend setting a reminder on your phone)
- Do ten squats every time you use the bathroom (trust me, this adds up!)

YOUR BODY WILL TELL YOU...

The way we treat ourselves is directly related to how we feel mentally. Sometimes, when our nutrition slips, when we stop moving our bodies, or when we have not dealt with an emotional issue, we fall into a downward spiral.

Your body will tell you when something is physically, spiritually, or mentally out of alignment. For me, if I feel out of control in one area of my life (or two, or three), my food issues bubble up. I'll find myself in the kitchen, mindlessly eating. It's a clear sign that there is something in my life I need to address. Some people drink too much, suffer from insomnia, or experience terrible stomach aches. Do not ignore the signs your body is giving you. Listen and listen closely!

If you are receiving these hints, it might be wise to look at the current structure of your life. I like having a predictable schedule. Knowing when I am going to exercise and what I am going to eat are helpful strategies to pull me back into the upward spiral.

Sometimes the fall into the downward spiral lasts only a day, but sometimes it's an entire season…

DISCOVERING A NEW VERSION OF ME

When I was twenty-five, I went to China and Thailand for a Rotary volunteer project. I flew across the ocean with my mom, my boss/mentor, and a high school student (who became a great friend). It was my first international trip, and we were going to teach English to schoolchildren.

(If you are unfamiliar with Rotary, it is an international service organization. Rotary's biggest claim to fame is the near eradication of Polio. Look them up and join a club! They are an amazing group!)

As I traveled around Asia, I realized that for the first time in a long time, I wasn't thinking about how many calories I was consuming and burning during the day. In fact, food and exercise didn't feel stressful at all. I was actually having fun! We were eating new things, and it all felt adventurous and delicious. We walked from our housing to the local school each morning and to many activities in the community.

Surrounded by new experiences and investing my time being of service to others took my mind off my own first-world problems. I mean, we were teaching at a school in southern China where the students had to exercise once an hour to keep warm because it was January and their school didn't have heat! How could I possibly think about my calorie count?!

This trip opened my eyes to how many blessings I had (and still have) in my life; blessings I didn't choose but was graciously born into. Traveling abroad helped me form a new relationship with my body and my health. It also shifted my perspective in a powerful way, and I knew there was no going back.

LET'S GET REAL FOR A SECOND

Can I safely assume that most of us have an issue or two with either our bodies or our health? There are things we don't like, things we want to change, and things we struggle with.

Being in Asia taught me to put my self-criticism in the back seat and make appreciation my preferred passenger. While I try to keep these priorities, the truth is, it's not always easy. I strive to maintain a healthy lifestyle, but sometimes life gets in the way and it becomes harder to keep guilt and shame at bay.

There will absolutely be seasons of your life when your nutrition and exercise take a backseat to your circumstances. Sometimes, we need to put simplicity at the top of the priority list. In those difficult or busy seasons, we can't always choose what is nutritionally best for our bodies, but there is still a choice to make. The choice comes in giving yourself a little grace and knowing when to let go.

When I started writing this book, I was nine months pregnant. As I type out my thoughts for this chapter, my second child—a beautiful daughter—is only a few weeks old. For me, pregnancy and the newborn phase are two seasons of life when I need to loosen my grip on nutrition. In fact, I found that eating to feed my child empowered me to free myself (in a new way) from past food obsessions. My nutrition was no longer about me. I knew that my body was going to change, and so I didn't worry as much as I normally would.

I learned to listen to what my body was asking for and to honor my cravings. Sometimes, I would stand in front of the fridge, and nothing looked appealing because I desperately wanted to eat potato chips. So, I'd listen and think, *my body probably needs salt.* Normally, I make sure to eat vegetables with my lunch and dinner, but in pregnancy, there was no way I wanted to eat a salad! I tried to incorporate vegetables as often as I could, but I also trusted that my baby was getting the nutrients she needed.

While this freedom to consume whatever my heart desired would normally be challenging for someone in recovery from an eating disorder, I comforted myself by remembering that these habits would only last for a specific amount of time—nine months of pregnancy, followed by a period of breastfeeding. This is certainly not how I want to eat for the rest of my life, but it's absolutely fine for now.

Maybe you are not eyeball deep in diapers like me but have been through seasons when your work, your family, or a creative pursuit needed to take priority and (most) all your attention. I have a cousin who, after law school and her first few years at a major firm, worked a ridiculous number of hours each week. She would often have breakfast, lunch, and dinner at her office. It seemed unreasonable for her to pack and take three full meals to the firm each day, and even if she was motivated to do so, she had limited time to grocery shop. Her priorities had to shift for a few years. If she ate a healthy breakfast or lunch, and then had takeout Chinese for dinner, so be it!

Sometimes, your health calls for self-compassion. You need to remember that life won't always be so chaotic or stressful (hopefully). Giving yourself permission to do whatever you need to do in order to survive is absolutely okay from time to time. Again, it's a season.

SELF-REFLECTION: HEALTH BY THE NUMBERS

- How many hours a week do you spend sitting at a desk or in front of the TV?
- How many hours a week do you spend outside?
- How many hours a week do you exercise?
- How many nights of the week do you eat dinner in front of the TV?
- How many items on your grocery bill are natural? How many are processed?

YOUR HEALTH SHOULD BE SUSTAINABLE

Life is constantly changing. You got a new job. You moved to a new town. You went through a breakup. You became a parent. You started college. In these times of transition, it's probably not a good idea to try and run a six-minute mile and qualify for the Olympic marathon, or to train for the next Ironman race. Sustainability is about looking at the current reality of your life and setting reasonable goals based on priorities. This mindset will keep you in the upward spiral.

Do you *really* need to exercise seven days a week, or is it more important that you get a good night's sleep?

Layering guilt upon failed expectations doesn't help anyone. As women, we are naturally good at shaming ourselves. One of the strategies I use to determine my priorities is creating an *Intolerables* List. For example, I dislike going longer than two days without getting outside and moving my body. My anxiety and stress level start to build up pressure. So, staying inside three days in a row is on my *Intolerables* List. I need to eat a substantial and healthy breakfast. I've learned that my body likes bacon and eggs in the morning, so skipping my first meal is intolerable.

Maybe for you, losing touch with your spirituality is intolerable. Perhaps giving up a guilty pleasure is intolerable. (Life is short!) For me, a life without ice cream is not worth living. Yes, I know frozen yogurt is always an option, but it's not the same! Having too many rules around food is also intolerable. I need options, freedom, and the ability to trust my own judgment.

Take a minute to think about your spiritual, mental, and physical health. What would you include on your *Intolerables* List?

THE INTOLERABLES LIST

_____

_____

_____

_____

_____

_____

_____

_____

_____

_____

Based on your *Intolerables* List, are there any immediate actions you need to take that can be added to your *Incompletes* List? What is currently missing from your life? What underlying issues need to be addressed?

For example, if losing touch with spirituality is intolerable, perhaps an action item on your *Incompletes* List is to reconnect with your preferred religious group or perhaps try a new church. Maybe you haven't been to see a doctor for a complete physical checkup in a few years. Perhaps you want to bring joy and exploration back into cooking, and you would like to try a new recipe (might I suggest playing around with sous vide or an instant pot). Would you like to try journaling? Add it to the list!

Take a minute to record action items regarding your physical, spiritual, and mental health on the following list:

THE INCOMPLETES LIST

_____

_____

_____

_____

_____

_____

_____

_____

_____

_____

Whatever your *Intolerables* and *Incompletes* may be, remember to be kind to yourself and make health a priority. Success and accolades mean nothing if you are not well enough to enjoy them.

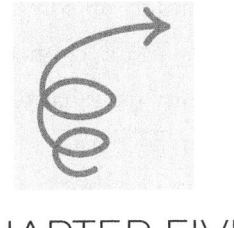

CHAPTER FIVE

TAKE CONTROL OF YOUR RELATIONSHIPS

My kindergarten teacher was an Australian woman who was very strict and harsh. She wasn't the typical nurturing, loving kindergarten teacher, and quite frankly, I was afraid of her. I was pretty sure she didn't like me. My five-year-old point of reference? One time I wrote on the whiteboard with the wrong kind of marker, and it was very upsetting for us both. Yet, at the parent-teacher conference, she spoke highly of me, saying, "Laurel is an all-arounder; she loves everyone. She wants to be friends with everyone, and she wants all her friends to get along."

To this day, that still rings true.

We live in a world with so much polarization, and we've lost sight of what it means to get along and respect one another. It's so disheartening because showing kindness should be such a normal practice. Smiling at someone, holding the door open…these small acts foster connection, which is a basic human need. (Like really, truly basic. I'm talking the second tier of "Maslow's Hierarchy" basic).

I don't know about you, but I aim to spend my life with people who encourage and elevate one another.

THE UPWARD SPIRAL

So much evidence supports having positive relationships in one's life. It's good for your mental health and helps you become whole, as a human being. For instance, a report out of the Mayo Clinic[7] suggests that having meaningful friendships increases happiness and a sense of belonging while reducing stress levels. Your relationships also have the potential to improve your self-confidence, to help you cope with trauma, and to motivate you to live a healthy life. And, get this…"Adults with strong social connections have a reduced risk of many significant health problems."[8] Who knew that surrounding yourself with good people could lower your blood pressure?!

Life is hard and you shouldn't have to do all the work on your own. We need to share the load (said in the voice of

---

7   https://www.mayoclinic.org/healthy-lifestyle/adult-health/in-depth/friendships/art-20044860
8   https://www.mayoclinic.org/healthy-lifestyle/adult-health/in-depth/friendships/art-20044860

beloved *Lord of the Rings* character Samwise Gamgee). With a village around us, we realize we are not alone. The more intentionally we work on keeping strong relationships in our lives, the easier it becomes to stay in the upward spiral, especially when life gets tough.

FRIENDSHIP IS A LEARNED SKILL

It takes a while (in life) to realize we have control over our relationships. When we are growing up, most of us spend time with our family, our teachers, our classmates, and our teammates. Perhaps you hung out with the kids of your parents' friends. There wasn't much choice about how we spent our time and who we were surrounded by. It wasn't all bad, though. We were growing our social skills during this stage, or so I tell myself.

Around the time we turn twelve or thirteen years old, we begin to develop an awareness about our relationships and begin to exercise choice. Sometimes, we enter into tougher relationships and need to learn how to navigate challenging dynamics. These are valuable experiences because they bring clarity. Knowing what *doesn't work* is an important thing and is perhaps easier to qualify than what *does work*.

Most of us tend to gravitate toward people who have similar energy and enjoy similar things. Motivational speaker Jim Rohn says that each person is the average of the five people they spend the most time with. Ideally, we want these to be high-caliber people, but that takes time to learn. We might not feel worthy of certain friendships or relationships due to our own self-esteem or limiting beliefs. Trust in the value you bring to a relationship, and take time to nurture the people you care about.

For me, intentionally forming intergenerational friendships is a key component of keeping me in the upward spiral. As an adult, I have friends who are both younger and older than me. Perhaps the eclectic group of people I enjoy dates back to my Rotary Club days. All kinds of people working closely together toward a shared goal. I loved hearing stories from people who were older and wiser than me. I also appreciated staying with host families when we traveled—learning their culture and language.

Being involved with Rotary also taught me the value of setting a good example for those who were younger than me. I got very close with the aforementioned student during our trip to China and Thailand. I was twenty-five, and she was still in high school, but we formed a really powerful relationship because with her, I felt free. I could totally be myself because, in her youth, she had no judgment about who I was or who I was supposed to be.

One of the problems these days (in my humble opinion) is that when we surround ourselves with people who look, think, and behave exactly like us, we perpetuate the same cycle of ideas. There is no exposure to new perspectives or life experiences. In having homogenous friend groups, we miss the joys of chatting with an elder, or mentoring someone younger.

To stay in the upward spiral, I strongly suggest you intentionally seek out friendships with people who are different from yourself. Seeing the world in a new way is a benefit.

Having someone challenge your ideas and beliefs makes you a better person. I'll admit, stepping outside of your comfort zone takes both skill and confidence. It is definitely not for someone who has relegated themselves to the passenger's seat.

GETTING IN THE DRIVER'S SEAT

The first step to getting in the driver's seat is gaining the confidence that you have a lot (or even a little) to offer another human being. I know this is easier said than done. Many of us have a running mantra of **I'm not good enough for this group. I don't fit in here.** But, if you consider that pretty much everyone else is feeling this same way, it levels the playing field.

When you become brave enough to put yourself out there (even when it feels uncomfortable), that's when the growth happens.

Every time I transitioned to a new school (elementary to middle school, middle to high school, high school to college), I was forced to build new friendships from scratch. Despite being young, I had enough wisdom to be choosy. I didn't just forge friendships with the person sitting next to me. I wanted to cultivate relationships with people I actually liked, and I continue to do so. (You know who you are.)

CULTIVATING POSITIVE RELATIONSHIPS

Strong relationships are formed with intentionality.

For me, that means carving out time to spend with someone, enjoying an activity together, making plans. In my friend group, I am often the one who brings all of us together, a role that is very important to me. As we get older and life starts to feel like controlled chaos—with work, marriages, and kids—I've come to realize that quality outranks quantity. I may not see my friends every week, but when we get together, it's meaningful and fun. We laugh. We discuss our goals, hopes, and dreams. We fill each other's buckets.

As for my primary relationship, my husband and I schedule a check-in twice a year. The sole purpose is to ask the other, "How's everything going? Are you happy? Do we need to switch anything up? What new goals do we have? How are you *really* doing?" We take an inventory of our life. It's far too easy *not to* have these discussions, and even more so with a toddler and a new baby. We have plenty going on, and we could easily forgo these dates and carry on with work and parenting. These conversations take effort, but they prevent resentment from building and eventually exploding. If left unsaid, small problems can become major ones over the course of time. Easy to avoid! Have the heart-to-heart.

I've made a habit of doing a mental check-in about the quality of all my relationships. **When was the last time I hung out with my friends? Have I done something nice for my spouse lately? Have I played with my kids? When was the last time I had my parents over for dinner? Are these things happening often enough?**

WAYS TO GAMIFY YOUR RELATIONSHIPS...

- Looking for new friends? See how many strangers you can talk to in a day. Make conversation in the grocery store, at school drop-off, in the coffee shop…you never know who you'll meet!
- Make a list of each relationship group (i.e., work relationships, family members, mom-friends, college friends), then choose one person from every group to connect with each month or even each week if your schedule allows (and you're an extrovert like me, haha!)

PRUNING TOXIC RELATIONSHIPS

It's no secret that as we age, we naturally get better at navigating relationships and finding people we want to spend time with. Sometimes, for a multitude of reasons, relationships are only meant to last for a season. People grow apart, they lose touch, they discover fundamental differences in each other. Other times, relationships become downright toxic.

There are people we meet whose negative energy can be felt a mile away. No, thank you! Just because someone shows interest does NOT mean you have to reciprocate or give yourself away. It's a good idea to come up with a litmus test when you meet new people, or a list of red flags that are non-negotiable. For example, I tend to shy away from people who misuse drugs/alcohol as this challenge generally spills over into all aspects of their life. I walk away from selfish people, who can't celebrate someone else's joy. People who make others feel bad about themselves out of jealousy or spite—not my jam. I also stay away from anyone who is competitive in an unhealthy way. You know the type—they think there are only so many slices of the pie, and they are unwilling to share.

My litmus test? If I don't feel like I can be myself around someone, they probably aren't for me.

Sometimes, a relationship starts off promising, but the vibe shifts and begins to feel negative. Being with this person is no longer joyful, but draining. If someone is not adding anything positive to your life or is costing you precious emotional energy, it may be time to prune them out. It's important to give yourself permission to do so. In these cases, I generally back away and let the relationship naturally fizzle out (passive approach) or give them the opportunity to become a better friend (active approach). Either way, I am in control of that relationship and whether I decide to continue being part of it.

Cloudy skies and negative people are the same. When they disappear, it is a brighter day.

I know that some toxic relationships are harder to extract yourself from, especially when it comes to family and work. This is where you need to establish strict boundaries to protect yourself. If you don't align politically with someone, for example, and this inevitably leads to an epic clash, perhaps you need to agree that the topic of politics is off limits. Other times, as hard as it is, you may need to grin and bear it.

My first professional mentor was a brilliant financial advisor, but a difficult person to please. You can imagine how challenging that was for the perfectionist in me! During the early days of becoming an advisor, I felt that I wasn't good enough to do the job, and I didn't get many words of affirmation to the contrary. Eventually, I realized that I couldn't count on my mentor's validation. I needed to trust that I did my best and make peace with the relationship I had with her. This job was important to my career, and I both wanted and needed to stay.

I did, however, ask myself how long I was willing to suffer in this situation, and I gave myself a timeline of when I could respectfully move on. Knowing this complicated relationship would not be a part of my life forever helped me cope on a daily basis.

THE POWER OF SAYING NO

You might think that saying *yes* is the key to being in control of your life. However, the true power lies in the ability to recognize what does *not* fill your bucket and establish healthy boundaries. If it doesn't bring you happiness or satisfaction, don't do it. Full stop.

It's perfectly fine to start small with this powerful habit. Maybe you turn down an offer for a drink with a coworker you don't enjoy. Perhaps you say no to having coffee with an old friend who no longer lights you up inside. You don't go to your in-laws' for dinner *every* Sunday. You turn down the request to be the manager of your kid's soccer team.

N.O. Those are two mighty letters! Slowly but surely, you will regain control of your time and who you spend it with.

Sometimes, boundaries sound like, "Yes, but…"

> **Yes, I will come to dinner, but I will only bring buns instead of a full entree.**
>
> **Yes, I will join you, but I need to leave at 8:30.**
>
> **Yes, I will help, but I don't have time until next week.**

If you can interject a smidgen of control in the situation, you might be preserving your precious sanity. Establishing this type of boundary keeps you in the upward spiral.

SELF-REFLECTION: RELATIONSHIPS BY THE NUMBERS...

- On average, how many times a week do you spend saying "yes" when you really want to say no?
- How much time do you spend each week on projects you have said "yes" to, which make you miserable?
- How many times have you gone out with a girlfriend in the last three months?
- How many times have you gone out on a date with your significant other in the last six months?

If you take anything away from this chapter, I hope it is this: Relationships are nurtured through intentionality. They take effort.

It's so easy to become complacent—to keep hanging out with a person who makes you feel bad about yourself because you are scared to hurt their feelings or because you have so much shared history. Complacency lives in relationship purgatory—maybe you are not in the downward spiral, but you are not flying free in the upward spiral either. The older we get, the more we realize the beauty of cultivating relationships that help us evolve and grow. Let's finish this chapter by taking a moment to become intentional about who we need to walk away from (our *Intolerables*), who we want to reconcile with (our *Incompletes*), and who we need to express gratitude to (our *Completes*).

As an example, my *Intolerables* would be:

- Selfish people
- People who don't lift one another up
- People who misuse drugs or alcohol
- People who don't like nature

THE INTOLERABLES LIST

My *Incompletes* would be:
- Reconnecting with an amazing friend I lost touch with, both being so caught up in the business of life
- Thanking my high school English teacher for inspiring me to write
- Anyone whose feelings I have hurt (either accidentally or intentionally)
- Anyone who has fallen off my radar that I would like to rekindle a relationship with

THE INCOMPLETES LIST

And, bonus for this chapter...

THE COMPLETES LIST

Take a moment to express gratitude for the following humans:
- Who makes you laugh?
- Who has gifted you with an act of kindness lately?
- Who has comforted you in the past?
- Who makes your life easier?
- Who is a joy to be around?

CHAPTER SIX

TAKE CONTROL OF YOUR FINANCES

In my earliest childhood memories, I was aware that my family had limited means—we weren't dirt poor, but we weren't rich either. We had a cute little house and two used cars. I remember one winter the heat failed in the two-door Toyota Corolla, so my brother and I wore snowsuits. Inside the car. All winter long. (I guarantee they were one-piece snowsuits, most likely neon because: the early '90s). Although this experience made me think we truly were poor, I realize in hindsight that my parents made the conscious choice to work less so they could have more time with us—they chose having time over having money. This shifted as my brother and I got older, and our parents grew in their careers. No doubt we were fortunate.

My first job, at age sixteen, was in an ice cream shop. Truly it was a lot of fun—the kind of place where you sang for tip money (or got tipped to *stop* singing in some cases). I learned valuable lessons about people, life, and diversity working there. It helped me grow up. The most powerful memory, however, was the feeling of freedom and independence that came with my paycheck. I loved the sense of control in knowing the money was mine to do whatever I wanted. It was immensely gratifying.

Having my own money felt like a tangible step toward becoming an adult. Feeling the importance of this responsibility inspired me to make a point of becoming familiar with money. If I made seven dollars an hour, I wanted to know how much of that was taken out for taxes. How much money actually went into my pocket? Even as a teenager, I craved an awareness of how the financial world worked.

When I entered college, it was with the intention of studying environmental economics. I cared about the environment and wanted to save the world, but I wasn't a super sciency person, so that wasn't the route for me. Instead, I found myself learning more and more about the economy and naturally transitioned into business. In Alaska, the majority of economics jobs are related to the fishing and oil industries—neither of which interested me. My parents worked with a financial advisor, and my dad would mention him from time to time. He introduced me to the idea of a Roth IRA, which made me stop and think about the importance of my own financial future.

(A Roth IRA is a type of tax-advantaged individual retirement account to which you can contribute after-tax dollars[9]. If you are not familiar with a Roth IRA, it is absolutely worth learning about!) The Roth has a special place in my heart as it was the very first investment I made (literally).

During my final semesters of college, a friend forwarded me an email from a member of her Rotary club looking for a financial advisor's assistant. Seeing as I was the only person to show up for an interview, I got the job! I ended up loving it, and my career path came into focus. (Cool side note: This friend is someone I met in an eating disorder recovery group, which reaffirms my belief that the lowest parts of my journey led to the most amazing successes. All things happen for a reason.)

OVERCOMING YOUR FEAR

We all have a relationship with money that is often formed in early childhood and through generations of societal messaging. Over the years, I've witnessed firsthand a pattern that female clients fear they will end up as bag ladies, no matter how much money they have. Women fear that their financial stability will go away, and they will end up on the street.

I wonder if this fear is a result of generations of women not being allowed to access or manage their *own* money. Although some weren't given any financial education, they were (and are) often the ones responsible for paying the bills

---

9   https://www.investopedia.com/terms/r/rothira.asp

and keeping track of the family finances. It's only in recent history that women have gained sufficient earning power so as not to be reliant on their spouses for security. There's a disparity between the level of responsibility required for these tasks and the confidence we feel when executing them. Women are well equipped to run the household (financially and otherwise), but we still lack confidence when it comes to managing our own finances. We are absolutely competent, but it's not enough to dispel the deep-seated fear.

As much as my parents warned me against going into a social services type of career (bless you), in a roundabout way, that's where I ended up. Much of my job as a financial advisor is coaching women (and men) through their emotions, mistakes, and limiting beliefs when it comes to taking control of their finances.

Let's walk through a few of the most common hurdles I see.

1. A lack of financial awareness

When I work with younger clients (a.k.a. people my own age), I start by asking them where they would like to be in thirty years. We take a look at their current financial situation and build a plan to make their vision a reality.

We also play out the worst-case scenario—their spouse passes away, their pension is lost (ha, not that Millennials or Gen Zers are thinking about pensions), they lose a job...then I ask them how much money they need to have in their bank account in order to feel safe.

SELF-REFLECTION: FINANCES BY THE NUMBERS...

- How much money is currently in your bank accounts?
- How much money do you owe on your credit cards?
- How much money do you need in a "rainy day fund" to feel secure?
- How much money would you like to save for retirement?

Learning to take control of your finances requires time and education. I understand that not everyone is in the position to hire a financial advisor, and I do not want to come across as tone deaf. The fact that someone can hire me means they already have a certain level of privilege. Despite this, I hope all readers are able to gain something from this section. After years of working as a professional in this field, I have learned many things and have many thoughts. I'd love to share a few simple steps you can take to increase your financial awareness.

- If you are not the one who pays the bills, start asking questions about the allocation of money.
- Take a look at your bank and credit card statements to see where the majority of your money goes. How much of that spending is required (mortgage/rent, groceries, gas),

> and how much of it is desired (shopping, entertainment, eating out)?
> - Know how much money is in your bank accounts.

I challenge you to take one step toward making a change. Small steps lead to substantial improvements (over time) in your sense of confidence and control.

2. Limiting your career potential

Complacency will keep you in the downward spiral every single time. If you are not happy with your financial situation, don't be a victim! Imagine different possibilities and then build a plan to get there. Perhaps that means exploring new career options with higher earning potential. Maybe it means considering the place you currently live in terms of affordability.

The simplest three-part formula when thinking about making changes to your financial situation is:

1. Ask yourself what you love and what you are good at
2. Explore how you might make money doing that
3. Develop, improve, and nurture your skillset(s)

I recently started following a woman on social media who loves reality television. She was familiar but not adept at Microsoft Excel. She dedicated time and self-taught Excel to an impressive level of proficiency. Once there, she combined her interest (reality TV) with her skills (Excel) and decided to make these amazing graphs and charts about different shows and post them online. She also teaches classes on how to become an Excel wizard, so she created not one, but TWO viable businesses! (#girlboss).

We are living in a world that offers a variety of creative and flexible careers. We also live in an era where education is more accessible than ever. You can listen to podcasts, read books, take online courses, and watch YouTube videos.

When I talk to clients about making a career change, I encourage them to think about their natural inclinations as a child. What were their skills and interests? Where did they shine in elementary school? As weird as it is, these early passions usually stick with us throughout life and can hint at a new career path.

As a kid, I loved math. I was also very good at connecting with people and was a natural cheerleader, always wanting others to succeed. Those skills absolutely transfer into my career as a financial planner. Maybe you loved to draw and build. Architect! Did you love reading and writing? Editor! And, when you find that job that makes you smile, don't be afraid to go for it!

I strongly encourage you to apply for any job that interests you, even if you don't meet all the qualifications. One of the top hindrances to women in the workplace is ourselves! We do not apply for jobs unless we meet most of the requirements. Men, on the other hand, do not subscribe to that limiting belief. *Harvard Business Review* posted a statistic stating, "Men apply for a job when they meet only 60% of the qualifications, but women apply only if they meet 100% of them."[10]

Whaaat?!

Be confident and own your potential! The worst they can say to you is "no" and then you are no worse off than you currently are. Maybe, just maybe, you'll surprise yourself and get the job, but if you don't even apply, you've robbed yourself of the chance. You've created a self-fulfilling prophecy.

I truly believe if you are motivated and confident, you could walk into any business and ask for a job. If someone walked into my office and presented nicely, introduced themselves and said, "Hey, I'm a hard worker, and I'm really interested in this field. Is there any way I could intern or work in a position where I could learn more?" I would give that

---

10 https://hbr.org/2014/08/why-women-dont-apply-for-jobs-unless-theyre-100-qualified

person the opportunity. I think all businesses can grow by hiring quality human beings.

My business partner and I hired a woman who did precisely this. She approached me with an interest in cultivating a financial advisory career and, since Day One, has done incredible things. Now *she* is the one bringing new ideas to the table!

Recently, a friend of a friend called me expressing interest in financial planning as a career choice. Although I didn't have the capacity to hire him myself, I referred him to another group in town that I highly respect. He got a job with them.

It may feel scary to take a risk and put yourself out there. Remember, the worst they can say is: no. Be diligent, be proactive, talk to the right people (which is to say, the ones who are doing the things you hope to also do someday).

Finding a job you are excited about (not every day necessarily, but more days than not) is the best way to keep you in the upward spiral. If you are stuck in a limiting situation, you don't need to stay there forever. Get creative, explore your options, educate yourself, and take a chance to improve your financial future.

3. Not asking for what you are worth

Even those of us in our preferred careers can limit our potential by not asking for the compensation we deserve. We don't want to seem pushy or ungrateful, but these fears put a ceiling on earning potential. Don't be afraid to ask for what you are worth! (This can be extra challenging as an entrepreneur, because you are putting a value on yourself).

As women, we tend to ask, *why me?* I think we should change that vernacular to, *why NOT me?* (Thank you for the beautiful question, Mindy Kaling).

One of my close friends works for a nonprofit organization, which she loves but also puts a cap on her income potential. She worked hard and learned how to write grants, create graphic designs, and build her monetizable skillset. In essence, she became more valuable (I would even say invaluable) to her organization. When someone else left their role, my friend stepped up and said that she could take over those responsibilities as well as her current ones. The organization no longer needed to fill that empty position with another employee, freeing up some capital to go to my well-deserving friend.

If you love your job and want to increase your salary, it can be a good idea to find a mentor. Make an effort to connect with people in your community whom you admire, and ask them how they achieved success. Most people are happy to share and feel flattered to be asked. They can give advice about which skills to develop, who you need to form relationships with, and how to make yourself an asset to your organization.

Most of us sell ourselves short simply by not asking.

I've seen it with my own team! When we conduct annual reviews, I expect my employees to ask for a raise, and I'm shocked when they don't. I want them to ask for additional training or certification (and I'm more than willing to pay for it). In truth, it's cheaper for companies to train and promote from inside their organizations than it is to recruit and hire from the outside. Just ask!

Do you want more work-life balance and really wish you could work remotely part of the week? Just ask!

You need to be your number-one advocate. If you let fear hold you back, you are limiting your earning potential, job satisfaction, and general happiness. No bueno.

SACRIFICES

Okay, now that you have developed an awareness of your financial situation and you are making moves to better your career, we need to have a hard talk. There are only two ways to get more money in your bank account, 401(k), or vacation fund: MAKE MORE** or SPEND LESS.

There is always room for improvement when it comes to spending. Most of us spend more money than we realize on frivolous things with little to no ROE (remember, Return on Enjoyment). If we want to create a financial buffer to ease our fear of total ruin…if we want to save for a rainy day when the washing machine breaks down…if we want to make that dream vacation a reality, then we may need to make a few sacrifices here and there.

I'm not suggesting total scarcity or deprivation; I'm saying that aligning your priorities with your spending is important and can even be fun.

WAYS TO GAMIFY YOUR SPENDING...

- How many days per week can you ride your bike or take transit instead of driving? (This will save on gas and parking costs!)
- Set a goal and see if you can keep your credit card statement under a specific amount each month.
- One better, how much can you pay off on that credit card each month?
- Go out for dinner with your friends, but don't order an app, or skip that glass of wine.
- Set a budget and keep cash in an envelope. Work only from that cash. You can play around with it. Spend less on groceries and more on your date night. Have money left over at the end of the month? Buy yourself a little treat!

Don't forget to reward yourself once in a while! Financial starvation is not sustainable. You will eventually crumble and splurge! Have you ever been on a really strict diet and eaten nothing but cabbage soup for weeks, only to fall off the wagon and eat a whole cake? (I really hope not, but I'm going for shock value here). Well, this also happens when it comes to spending money. Set up a savings account and put a few dollars in whenever you can. Watch it accumulate and then spend it on something fun—a new shirt, a dinner out, a road trip.

WAYS TO CREATE WEALTH (**MAKE MORE)

There are only so many ways to cut spending; therefore, making more money is the preferred solution. I mean this in two ways—increase your income where possible and invest that income. Earning money *on* your money will have an exponential impact on your future, so let that sink in.

One of the best ways to grow your wealth is to invest in the stock market. Let's preface this section by admitting that investing in individual stocks takes a certain amount of knowledge and guidance. For the sake of this book, we are going to keep things high-level. I want to stoke your curiosity so that you feel inspired to go out and learn more. I also want to show you what is possible.

Investing has never been more accessible. There are so many do-it-yourself platforms available (which is great and also scary.) My advice to those new to investing is to start boring and stay boring. The best way to grow your money is to invest in well-established companies that have a strong track record. Crypto might sound cool and appealing, but there are a lot of unknowns. The same goes for emerging markets.

"Boring" looks like an S&P 500 index fund, which is the group of stocks representing the 500 biggest companies in the United States. While some of them are highly correlated (the tech industry, for example), you are also getting exposure to other industries. These companies will change over time as the top-500 list evolves, and this is a good thing. For instance, there weren't many science and tech options twenty years ago.

Regardless, as the companies in the S&P 500 continue to grow, your money will too (if you choose to invest in them).

My second piece of advice is "don't chase past performance." How a stock has done in the past is not a guarantee of future results. If a company is doing great on the market today, it does not mean it will be doing great tomorrow. Investing takes patience. Even if some of those S&P 500 stocks take a dip for months at a time, don't panic! In fact, celebrate those dips by "buying low" and wait it out for long-term appreciation.

Now, I can imagine some of you saying, "That's great, Laurel, but I don't have money to invest in the stock market."

I'm not naive. I won't sit here and tell you that if you stop buying lattes, you will magically be able to afford a house. We both know that's not going to happen. So…let's think a little bigger. Pick one guilty pleasure you are willing to let go of. Everyone has something—buying new clothes, streaming services, ordering DoorDash. Take that money and put it in the stock market instead. I will never forget the powerful phrase: **set it and forget it**, which means automating your savings, contributions, investments, etc., so you don't have to think about it. It just happens. Because a set amount is automatically transferred, it reduces the temptation to *not* contribute each month. ("Well, I really want that new [insert object of desire here], so I'll transfer double next month instead." Yeah, right!)

I want you to live a joyful life and not be stuck in a paycheck-to-paycheck situation where you are barely making ends meet. By examining your relationship with money, developing an awareness, and then allowing yourself to reach your full potential, you will gain control over your financial future. You will grow in confidence and begin living in the upward spiral of life.

FINAL REFLECTIONS

What financial and/or professional *Incompletes* do you have? A career option you never explored? A desire you never asked for? Education that could be helpful? Debts that should be paid?

THE INCOMPLETES LIST

When it comes to your career and your financial situation, what feels *Intolerable* to you?

THE INTOLERABLES LIST

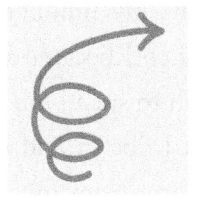

CHAPTER SEVEN

TAKE CONTROL OF YOUR TIME

Kate Spade is credited to have said, "Live colorfully." It's printed on the tags of her clothing line, and it seems to be an amazing motto for how to live a good life. I choose to take this literally (and figuratively), to bring vibrance into my world by getting out of my daily rut and becoming intentional about how I spend my time. I want to talk to interesting people, take risks, and have adventures—big and small. To do this, I need to step back every once in a while and discover what is preventing me from living colorfully, to analyze what in my life is no longer serving me. Like spring cleaning my closet, sometimes I need to make space and reassess my priorities so I can spend my time doing things that fill my bucket.

Priorities are really the crux of this chapter, which determine how you take control of your time. Our priorities ebb and flow depending on the season of life we are in. That's why assessment is not a one-and-done task.

There were periods of my life when training for various athletic pursuits became my number one priority, therefore absolutely necessary. Then I became a mother. In my current season, I no longer wish to spend ten hours a week marathon training. While I want to be fit and healthy, I don't want to take too much time away from my family. My competitive nature has slid further down my priority list. Maybe I'll get back there one day, and most likely in another area of my life.

Time is a precious resource, one that we can't create more of. In order to fulfill all your roles and still have time to live colorfully, you need to be intentional. Balance does not happen by accident.

What is most important to you?

What are you willing to let go of?

FINDING YOUR BALANCE

We only have so much free time, so we need to find value where we can, in the moments that we have. When I am driving to the office, for example, I try to fill that time with something meaningful. I listen to an audiobook or a podcast. Or I use hands-free calling (safety first!) to talk to my mom or friends living out of state.

I really admire my former coworker (and current friend) who works a nine-to-five desk job, and has figured out a system that allows her to leave the office at the end of the day and be fully present with her family when she gets home. Each week, she plans her one-hour lunch break with precision. One day, she goes to the grocery store. Another day, she runs errands. She'll meet me for lunch once in a while. Because she is deliberate and organized, when she gets home, she can relax and focus on the "fun stuff." Best of all, her weekends are free and clear to go camping and explore!

If I'm being totally honest, because I have my own business, the boundaries between work and home can get blurry. For this reason, I've had to create a set of rules I try to abide by, which allow me to be present when I am with the people I love. Here's my game-changing (and super helpful) life hack: Move your work email to its own screen on the last page of your apps. This way, you only see your email if you *choose* to look for it by swiping all the way to the end [insert swipe right joke here]. I also try not to check my phone during family time, especially when we are eating dinner together (the operative word here is "try"—it's a work in progress). Family moments are precious, and I want to be fully present.

GUILT. IT'S REAL.

Guilt is inherent to having the second X chromosome.

If you are a woman, chances are you frequently experience guilt when it comes to how you spend your time. We feel guilty when we are at work because we should be home with our families. We feel guilty at home because there is so much work to do. We arguably feel the most guilt whenever we choose to spend time doing something for ourselves.

Getting over the guilt takes practice. Each time I choose to do something just for me, I think of it as a little act of rejuvenating rebellion.

When the guilt creeps in, I remind myself that the time I give to myself is going to make me feel great. If I want to be a positive partner, a patient parent, a productive business owner, then I need to be at my best. My family is going to be okay. My work is going to be okay. Everything will be there when I return. I like to imagine this moment is frozen in time, and the rest of the world is hovering in stillness. I'll get my nails painted for forty-five minutes, and then everything will return to being the way it was before I "disappeared" for *me* time.

I don't agree with most things Kim Kardashian does or says, however I heard her share in an interview that she is religious about her morning skincare routine for her face. If her skin looks good, it gives her confidence throughout the day. As much as it pains me to say, I agree with Kim K on this. I believe in this principle. If we take time to do something for ourselves that makes us feel good (and/or look good in this case), it helps us get into the upward spiral. It might give us the edge we need to slay the day.

To get over the guilt, I had to take control and be intentional about flipping the script.

It is so easy to push off our own self-care, but we ultimately never recover it. For me, it all comes back to my health. I need to protect this time if I want to be the best version of myself in this world and show up for everyone else.

THE SOCIAL MEDIA VORTEX

Has there ever been a bigger time suck than social media?

We can easily waste hours of time being pulled into a continuous loop of comedy videos and influencers' posts. I could waste a whole day watching clips from *The Office*! My ribs would be hurting too…

The thing is, if you are not careful, spending too much time on social media can be a one-way ticket into the downward spiral.

None of us are ever going to be as pretty as…, as athletic as…, as rich as…, as stylish as…. This increases our feelings of depression, unworthiness, FOMO, etc. As a new mother to a baby daughter, I am keenly aware of the statistics on the alarming rates of depression in teenage girls and the correlation to social media.

You need to tailor your social media to be a positive reflection of the world. What you scroll should serve you in some way—inspire and uplift you. If it doesn't, hit *unfollow*!

I think we also need to be aware of the amount of time social media consumes on a daily basis. It's not a bad idea to set a timer or to establish rules around your usage.

I check my social media in the bathroom. Is that terrible? I'm not even a little embarrassed because I have a newborn and a toddler. Momma needs her time! Where else am I going to watch clips from comedy shows, uninterrupted? It gets awkward with my family…they're always asking, "Where did Mom go? Is she okay in there?" Regardless, this rule keeps my social media scrolling to a minimum. I can't hang out on the potty forever.

There are also apps that track your screen time and can even break it down to the specifics. How many hours per week are you Googling, emailing, Instagramming, or TikToking?

Gently remind yourself of your priorities. If you know having screen time before bed leads to not sleeping well, don't do it! The repercussions felt the next day are simply not worth it.

SELF-REFLECTION: TIME BY THE NUMBERS...

- How much screen time do you average per day?
- How much time do you spend commuting? (How can you leverage this time?)
- How many times do you do something nice for yourself in an average month?
- How many hours do you spend volunteering or helping others?

WHERE YOU SPEND YOUR TIME

Most of us spend a large chunk of our week at work, yet we don't always make our workspace a reflection of ourselves.

Research shows a direct correlation between mental health and our physical environment[11]. We are affected by aesthetics such as color and tidiness, as well as sensory factors such as noise, lighting, and smells. It doesn't take much to improve your environment in small ways, which can bring you more joy and satisfaction on a regular basis.

---

11   https://www.verywellmind.com/how-your-environment-affects-your-mental-health-5093687

Let's say you work in a cubicle. Do you have some color? Family photos? A vision board or a quote that inspires you? What you see throughout the day can bring you into the upward spiral.

I was resistant to live plants for a long time (yeah, I'm talking about those lovely green things that need sunlight and water to survive). They're a pain, and I don't know how to keep them alive. While that's still mostly true, I've learned to love succulents. They are low maintenance and very pretty to look at. It's a small addition to my environment that brings me joy.

I also have a slight obsession with colorful containers (boxes, totes, folders, you name it). I use them to organize my surroundings and minimize the clutter. As an added bonus, their rainbow hues make me smile.

There's a reason why Marie Kondo is so popular (in addition to her being absolutely adorable). While extreme minimalism is not always necessary, it is very important to keep your space tidy. If your work environment is a mess, it can be hard to focus. You'll be easily distracted, and the disorganization will nag at you. When things are tidy, we feel refreshed and energized. There's a science behind it!

This goes for your home as well. If you are constantly looking for your misplaced phone or keys, you are certainly not maximizing your time. Having a specific spot for things and keeping them in their proper place makes your day painless.

When it comes to organizing my home, one of the best lessons I learned relates to "prime real estate." The only items that occupy my countertops (especially in the kitchen) are ones I use on the daily. While my salt and pepper shakers take up prime real estate, the ice cream maker I use twice a year goes into the storage closet. Who am I kidding? I probably haven't used that thing in five years! Time to donate.

I hope you are hearing my message. Your physical environment, where you spend your time, impacts your mental health.

Tip: Organize your closet one category of clothing at a time. Go through your workout clothes, then your pants, followed by your t-shirts, etc. Challenge yourself to donate at least five items of clothing per category during this process. Repeat every season.

IT'S NOT A COINCIDENCE

This may sound a bit woo-woo, but hear me out…

When my husband and I were trying to conceive our first kiddo, we were having trouble. It was taking a really long time. We were stressed, disappointed, and feeling overwhelmed from doing everything we could to make it happen. Not to mention my Type A personality told me I should "get it right" the first time. HA!

One of the things I felt we needed to do was create a nursery, so I hired a housekeeper to help organize our space. The room we intended to use was a cluttered, chaotic storage/art/guest room/random space. This wonderful woman (a hippie stoner musician) came and helped me clean out the bedroom. We moved some items, put others into storage, and threw a lot away. (Very much like the Marie Kondo methodology, but I didn't hold everything in my hand and ask if it brought me joy).

When we finished the project, the woman hugged me and said, "I think you'll be able to get pregnant now."

She was right. I got pregnant the next month. Before this moment, the room held no purpose. It wasn't serving us or our mental health. It felt like chaos and disorder. As soon as I reorganized the space, it felt like we were getting ready for the future.

THE CHOICE IS NOT ALWAYS EASY

I once had a manager who didn't have my best interests at heart. Being new-ish to the business world, it was a tough thing to wrap my brain around. In my early twenties, I thought everyone would care about me and help me—and he was not that way. I did not want to spend my time around him. Once I recognized that I couldn't trust him, I quickly decided to physically relocate my business.

Though I knew it was the right choice, it was definitely scary to go out on my own. Working with a fantastic therapist gave me the added confidence to make the move. Three cheers for talk therapy: hip hip hooray!

Life has a way of offering you beautiful surprises, if you have the guts to make the brave choice. Leaving that communal office gave me tenfold benefits on my ROE! It gave me a greater sense of independence. It allowed me to design and decorate my office space the way I wanted. Most importantly, owning my own company allowed me to influence the lives of women in my community by hiring and nurturing talent. It was so exciting! My team today is a big reason I look forward to going to work.

Although initially terrifying, the whole experience was empowering as I saw my dream vision come to life. Taking control of who I spent my workday with and where I spent my time, as well as focusing on who I could help, all lead to a profound awakening.

GAMIFY YOUR ORGANIZATION

- I love the idea of having a calendar and dedicating each month to purging a specific area of your house. January is the kitchen. February is the pantry. March is the laundry room. I am a strong believer in having a system; otherwise we defer or skip it, and nothing ever gets done. When was the last time you cleaned out your spice rack/drawer/cupboard, by the way?

LIVING COLORFULLY

Now that you have re-evaluated your priorities and organized your life both physically and mentally, you may find yourself with available brain space to imagine a life colored with adventure.

Your time should not solely be dedicated to work, to connection, and to self-growth. You also need to be intentional about creating time to play!

Adventure is the word I use to categorize something as simple as trying a new restaurant in town or as audacious as planning an Antarctic vacation. (For the record, as wild as going on a voyage to Antarctica sounds, I have no desire to be that far south. Shoot, you've got to draw the line somewhere!)

Each of us has a spectrum for adventure, things small and large that push us out of our comfort zone. You don't even need to try a new restaurant! Maybe you eat something new off the menu of your favorite place instead. Whatever you choose, adventure is about making your life bigger, getting out of your mundane routine, and allowing yourself to broaden your horizons. What's the next item on your bucket list?

As a kid, I didn't realize how lucky I was to be born into an adventurous lifestyle. It wasn't until I moved out of Alaska during college that I recognized the innate advantage of my surroundings. Hiking, playing in the snow, and having nature at my fingertips continually inspires me to seek new perspectives.

I'd love to travel, to visit one hundred countries. We don't know what we don't know, and we'll never discover the unknown unless we make an effort to find it. Perhaps you'll fall in love with a new style of architecture, or feel connected to the animals on the African safari. Travel can change you in ways I am certain sitting at your desk cannot.

I want to see the different ways people live, appreciate their ingenuity, and let it filter into my life back home. In Amsterdam, people ride their bikes everywhere. Maybe I can ride mine to work once in a while. Seeing the world outside of your town creates new neural pathways. Exposing yourself to different languages and cultures adds color to life.

Maybe you cannot afford travel right now, or it's not feasible during the season you are currently in. (I am envisioning a screaming baby and antsy toddler on a twelve-hour flight. I am not signing up for this until my kids are older). There are budget-friendly ways to experience the world. You could watch a program from *National Geographic*, listen to different kinds of music, search for recipes from around the globe. If you get creative and think outside the box, there are many ways to have adventures without jumping on an airplane.

The first step in creating time for adventure is to get out of autopilot, living every day as your own personal déjà vu. Shake it up! Incorporate something new into your regimen. Get spicy!

LIVING COLORFULLY MEANS BEING ADVENTUROUS WITH YOUR TIME

You don't need to live a life where you work from 8 a.m.–5 p.m. Your days off don't need to be Saturdays and Sundays. Society has gotten a lot more flexible in terms of how we work and live. If you value being home with your family, or traveling the world, then I encourage you to explore ways to work that don't confine you to an office or a desk. There is an abundance of new work structures that allow us to be intentional and adventurous with our time, giving us the freedom to live more colorfully.

Time is my most precious resource. When I am at work, my goal is to have meetings on my calendar with people I am excited to see. If I don't want to talk to this person, I really need to think about that because my time is valuable. Every meeting I have means I am choosing to be away from my family, to dedicate less time to adventure, to find less time for myself. My goal is to be purposeful and spend my time in a way that enriches my life, whether at work, at home, or out in the world.

IT'S REFLECTION TIME!

In terms of time, your *Incompletes* might be:

- An organization project
- An unfulfilled adventure
- A lack of time for self-care

THE INCOMPLETES LIST

Some of my *Intolerables* are:

- Minimal life-work balance
- Becoming complacent, a victim to circumstance (thinking my life can't be adventurous, or I can't possibly find time for myself)

THE INTOLERABLES LIST

CONCLUSION

Society has established certain metrics for measuring success and accomplishment. The sad thing is, some of us are innately set up for success because we fit into the boxes, while others are set up to "fail."

Take sports, for example. In the Olympics, there is a gold, silver, and bronze medal, but really only one winner. It leaves so many people out and discounts the incredible dedication and work they put in to even make the team. I was an athlete. I get the need to win, but I still hate seeing someone come in second place and feel like a failure. As a spectator, I am looking at those in second, fifth, and even last place and thinking, **Wow! In a million years, I could never surf a wave like you just did!** Yet, the athlete feels like they suck because they didn't win.

It's not right. There should be more celebrating.

We should celebrate second place, getting out of bed, finally washing your car, cooking a new recipe. However you want to celebrate—whether it be voicing your small victory to a friend, writing it down in your journal, or dancing in your closet—you should take the time to acknowledge the win. It gives you a hit of dopamine and changes your brain chemistry.

Many of us get caught up in feeling as if we should be doing better, like we are not enough. This thought pattern pulls us into the downward spiral. It's so easy to become derailed and defeated. The truth is, most of us are not going to win a gold medal, get straight A's, or become a CEO. So, we need to come up with a new measurement for success.

SUCCESS IS NOT A ONE SIZE FITS ALL

I think there is value in taking control of your own definition of accomplishment. It's important to figure out what your recipe for success is, in the context of your life. We are all unique individuals, and our goals shouldn't be the same. For one, painting a picture might feel like an accomplishment. For another, it could be running a five-mile race. For me, it might be finishing a financial plan that allows my client to retire early. For you, it will be something else entirely. We don't want to live in a homogeneous population. There's not a lot of color in that!

Once you decide what success looks like, then you need to come up with a plan that allows you to lean into your strengths instead of feeling bad about your deficits. Take stock of what you are good at and decide how you can use that to gain momentum toward the upward spiral.

For example, at the beginning of my career, success was landing a job as a financial advisor and growing in competence and confidence. During my first few years, I was mentored by a man and a woman, both of whom were very different from me. The fact that I wasn't similar in approach bumped up against my self-esteem. I felt like I wasn't good enough or wasn't cut out for this role.

Being younger, I was definitely more casual and wanted a personal relationship with my clients. I did (and continue to do) things differently, like sitting with people at a round table—which invites collaboration and equality—rather than sitting behind a desk. I didn't want clients to feel like they were in the principal's office and I was scolding them for spending too much money. My mentors, on the other hand, took a more hierarchical approach. They were the ones clients paid for good advice. Ultimately, though, the choice to follow that good advice was theirs.

After a few years on the job, I realized that I had unique gifts. I can simplify complex ideas and deliver that information in an approachable way. I can nurture meaningful, long-term relationships based on mutual respect and liking one another as humans.

These are my strengths, and the fact that they made me different from my mentors was a good thing. Clients continued working with me! The best thing I could aim to be was myself, and this actually helped me achieve my goal of establishing an enjoyable and fruitful career.

SETTING GOALS

Listen, the fact that this book is encouraging you to take control of your health, relationships, finances, and time doesn't escape me. These are no small feats! Knowing that, I want to set you up for success (your version, not mine) in whatever changes you choose to make in your life. So, if you will be kind enough to indulge me, I have some advice…

1. Share your goal with others

If your goal is to eat healthier, get a promotion, or incorporate some "me time" into your life, tell someone about it. Letting people know what you are working toward has a big impact.

First of all, it alleviates that awful guilty feeling of having to say no to invitations because you've already explained where your focus is. You want to honor yourself by pursuing that instead of becoming distracted by social obligations.

Second, by sharing, you are inviting support from those who love you. Maybe they will put out healthier snacks at the Super Bowl party, offer to babysit your kids so you can focus on your online coursework, or remind you of the reasons you are sacrificing.

Lastly, sharing your goals adds an extra layer of accountability. There is something powerful about speaking your goals out loud, to others. It brings your desire out of the abstract and into reality, often inspiring you to take action.

2. Set smaller, attainable goals

There's a theory of motivation that states many people who have big, lofty goals easily become discouraged because their dreams feel unattainable. However, if you take these big goals and break them down into bite-size achievable goals, the success you experience and celebrate along the way will increase your motivation. How do you eat a whale? One bite at a time. When you set out to hike Mount Everest, you don't just fly to Nepal and go for it. You train slowly. First a five-mile hike, then a ten-mile....

If you want to save money for a vacation, set a monthly goal and celebrate when you hit that number every thirty days. That's the reason I sprinkled all the gamification suggestions throughout the book. I want you to celebrate the tiny wins and train your brain to understand that even the most minuscule droplets accumulate to form a large puddle.

Creating sustainable change comes with time, effort, and patience. It doesn't happen overnight.

3. Use past accomplishments as fuel for the future

Do you remember when we discussed "the gap and the gain" at the beginning of this book? Looking back at how far you've come and what you have achieved can give you confidence to pursue future goals.

When I look back at my life, I am so proud that I graduated from college in the midst of my eating disorder. I needed to gain control of my health and remain dedicated to my education. I knew that was going to be a very important step in my life and career. It was really, really hard, but I did it.

Now, when I think of that twenty-something-year-old version of me, I can see she had grit, determination, and perseverance. When I am facing a challenge in my present life, I can draw upon that experience and remember that I have what it takes to do hard things.

Maybe you are having a difficult time using your past accomplishments as fuel for the fire. That's okay. If it's difficult for you to find inspiration in your own life, I wonder if you can find inspiration in those around you. I use my grandmother as a strong example for me. She moved to Alaska from rural Michigan at the age of twenty-three to become a secretary for the FBI. She came alone—traveled across the country, and got on a steamship in Seattle to arrive in Anchorage. She was the original brave woman in my life, and sometimes I think, *If she can do that, I can definitely do this.*

You *can* take risks. You *can* push yourself. You *can* explore a better way of living. You *can* be courageous.

And, you *can* get in the driver's seat and take control of your life.

EPILOGUE

I feel like it would be irresponsible to end this book without acknowledging that we each have our own strategies to cope with stress in an attempt to live our best lives. The suggestions I've made in this book are habits and mindsets that work for me, and I share them in the hopes they might work for you as well.

The truth is, I am far from perfect. [Im]perfect, actually, and proud of it!

I am still a work in progress. For example, I've read some pretty awesome information about the power of meditation and journaling. Do I want to incorporate those self-care habits into my daily routine? Yes! A thousand times, yes! Have I actually done it (for long enough to count)? No.

In this season of my life, nurturing my business, my marriage, and two small babies, I've accepted that there are only so many hours in the day. I can only take on so much! There are artworks I would love to create and ideas I'd like to explore. The day will come when I can add those habits back into my repertoire, but it is not today (or any time in the near future).

I'd love to hear about your self-care habits. If you meditate or journal, let's celebrate together. If you went on an epic hike, send me a picture. Let's create a community of women who are taking control of their lives.

Please reach out to me @laurelgai on Instagram (forgive me, I'm an elder millennial and haven't embraced TikTok…) or my website: www.laurelgai.com

Thanks for reading my book—now, go live colorfully!

Love,

Laurel

EATING DISORDER SUPPORT & RESOURCES

Eating Disorder Foundation Support Groups
www.eatingdisorderfoundation.org/get-help/support-groups/

Alliance for Eating Disorders Awareness Support Groups
www.allianceforeatingdisorders.com/recovery-programs-and-support/

ANAD Support Groups
anad.org/online-support-groups/

Ophelia's Place
www.opheliasplace.org/support-services

Multi-Service Eating Disorders Association (MEDA)
www.medainc.org/services/heal/medas-recovery-groups/

Eating Recovery Center
www.eatingrecoverycenter.com/support-groups

Eating Disorders Anonymous

eatingdisordersanonymous.org/meetings/

National Eating Disorder Association (NEDA)

www.nationaleatingdisorders.org/help-support/contact-helpline

The Emily Program

www.emilyprogram.com

And, as an added bonus: Doug Carter's coaching information!

www.dougcarter.com/solutions/coaching/

ACKNOWLEDGMENTS

I would like to thank the following bright lights for guiding me along this journey (so far)...
Mr. Paul Meredith for teaching me about people.
Ms. Jodette Knock for teaching me about numbers.
Mr. John Ruhlin for teaching me about writing.
Holly Brooks, Doug Carter, and Steph Figarelle for coaching and encouraging me.
Alex, Jo, and Maryn for helping me get help.
Emily Timmer for seeing and understanding me.
The Good Time Girls for knowing and loving me.
My brother, for making me laugh.
My spouse, for keeping me fed.
My dad, who quietly leads by example.
My mom, who is both my #1 fan and my #1 inspiration.
I love you all.

ABOUT THE AUTHOR

Laurel Renkert earned the nickname "Energizer Bunny" in high school. She is now on a mission to let people know that even Energizer Bunnies run out of batteries.

With her message of the upward spiral, Laurel aims to support women on their journey to take care of themselves and create their own happiness. She is an aspiring athlete and a wannabe interior designer. She is also an entrepreneur who specializes in financial planning.

Laurel lives in Anchorage, Alaska, with her husband and two delightful young children (one of whom was born during the writing of this book).

Made in the USA
Middletown, DE
31 December 2023